ABOUT THIS BOOK

"April 8, 1945, it was my birthday. I was 21. It was many months since we blew out of the sky into this God forsaken place."

Karnig Thomasian was the last crewman to parachute from his burning B-29 Superfortress that was in a flat spin with three engines and forward bomb bay on fire.

He landed and was immediately surrounded by Japanese soldiers. Life in the prison camp was one of being beaten with unyielding teakwood clubs, having dysentery and malaria, eating maggot-infested rice, but Karnig clung to life.

This book will show how a very bad decision by a base commander drastically affected the lives of 47 combat airmen.

Never underestimate the strength of the human spirit!

THEN THERE WERE SIX

The true story of the 1944 Rangoon Disaster, when only one of eleven B-29s returned to its home base. The cost...eighteen men killed, twenty-nine men captured by the Japanese, and ten B-29s destroyed. This is also a story of what happened to the twenty-nine POWs of the Japanese.

KARNIG THOMASIAN

authorHOUSE®

AuthorHouse™
1663 Liberty Drive
Bloomington, IN 47403
www.authorhouse.com
Phone: 1 (800) 839-8640

Published by AuthorHouse 09/23/2016

ISBN: 978-1-4184-4931-5 (sc)
ISBN: 978-1-4184-4930-8 (hc)

Library of Congress Control Number: 2004093463

Print information available on the last page.

Any people depicted in stock imagery provided by Thinkstock are models,
and such images are being used for illustrative purposes only.
Certain stock imagery © Thinkstock.

This book is printed on acid-free paper.

Because of the dynamic nature of the Internet, any web addresses or links contained in
this book may have changed since publication and may no longer be valid. The views
expressed in this work are solely those of the author and do not necessarily reflect the
views of the publisher, and the publisher hereby disclaims any responsibility for them.

THIS BOOK IS DEDICATED TO:

Five of my crew who did not get out of plane #831.
1st.Lt. Wayne 'Doc' Treimer, Pilot
Cpl. Vernon Henning, Central Fire Control
Cpl. Leon McCutcheon, Right Gunner
Cpl. Augie Harmison, Tail Gunner
Cpl. Robert Dalton, Radar Operator

1st.Lt. Hallouran Soules - plane #225
    Died soon after his plane
    landed at our base in Chakulia, India.

All men on plane #726 who died in the disaster.
Capt. Howard L. Gerber, Pilot
1st Lt. Robert W. Conway, Co-Pilot
1st Lt. Stacey B. Hall, Navigator
1st Lt. Charles Lancaster, Bombardier
1st Lt. Irving Burness, Flight Engineer
2nd Lt. Roy B. Allen, Radar Operator
T/Sgt. James A. Vermillion, Tail Gunner
S/Sgt. Theodore A. Birkmaier, Radio Operator
Sgt.   William T. Blank, Central Fire Control
Sgt.   Chester L. Cummins, Right Gunner
Sgt.   Allen J. Rice, Left Gunner
Sgt.   James M. McCarthy, who went on this mission
                        as an observer.

Contents:

ACKNOWLEDGMENTS

My wife, **Diana,** has my undying gratitude for encouraging me persistently for years to fulfill my dream of writing this book and for her many editing sessions; I also thank the late **Col. Ira Mathews,** who shared with me his intimate knowledge of the Rangoon disaster; **Norman Larsen,** my navigator, and **Nicolas Oglesby,** CFC gunner on Captain Shanks' crew, for sharing their accounts of the march from Rangoon; **Arnold Lang,** my computer guru, a generous, wonderful man, in whose debt I will always be for selflessly helping me with my computer problems night or day for years; **Barry Sheinkoph,** for the final and most crucial editing; **Bernadette Wolff,** a dear friend and writer, for her keen observations; **Aaron Elson** for sharing his knowledge in writing and producing books. He also introduced me to **Janet Kroenke** who lovingly used her computer expertise to produce the cover of this book per my layout. To **Kurt Heiman** for his incisive input on the graphics of the dust jacket. **Michael Lombardi,** historian of the Boeing Company, for two photos used in this book (pages 5 and 6); **George Ratcliffe,** British 2nd Battalion, K.O.Y.L.I., for use of three of the many drawings which the Japanese allowed him to make (pages 38, 46, and 87); **William A. Rooney**, 40th Bomb Group for his wealth of information and counsel; **Matt Poole** historian and fabulous researcher and friend for sharing his knowledge.

My drawings are on pages 49, 75, 82, and (Tarzan) 130.

PREFACE

I agonized over writing this book for many years until I decided on what I was going to write about. It wasn't enough to only describe my POW experience. I decided to uncover what had been tearing at me from my subconscious all those years. It was all about the mission, my last mission. It was about how a very bad decision from a commanding officer could have had such a dramatic impact on the lives of forty-seven men. Through the years, I had gathered documented information about that mission, some of which I have included in this book.

I could not, in all good conscience, live out my life without documenting this story. Now, at last, I am at peace.

I was a young man of eighteen the day I went off to war, and naive as the day is long. I was born in Manhattan, New York, in 1924, of Armenian descent. While I lived in a melting pot of Greeks, Italians,

Armenians, Irish, and Jewish people, I had sparse knowledge of the Chinese, Japanese, German, Black, Spanish, and Indian cultures; nor did I have a deep understanding of other beliefs, differing lifestyles.

However, my parents gave me a healthy respect for all people. I remember, after all these years, an incident when I was a teenager of about fourteen, when a Jewish kid was being harassed by a white boy. It was obvious that the Jewish boy was no match for his tormentor. Along came a well-built Irish kid of about seventeen with sandy, curly hair, and a rough sort of guy. He sized up the situation and quickly stood between the two boys and told the white kid, "I'm not Jewish, but I will defend his right to be one." The white boy hesitated and finally walked away.

That happened sixty-five years ago, and it made such an impression on me that I remember it to this day. I admired that rough Irish character standing up and defending this defenseless Jewish kid whom he didn't know.

After the Crash, my father lost almost everything; he sold our house in Kew Gardens, Long Island, where I had grown up as an only child with an aunt and two uncles and two grandmothers living with us. We moved into an apartment in Washington Heights, Manhattan, and could only take my mother's mother with us. This is where I grew up. The thing that I remember most was how hard my father, Arsen, worked. He'd lost so much, yet he never complained and had a successful embroidery business which catered to quality clients. In the summer I would go downtown to his office to help in running errands. I remember one day I had to deliver a package to Henri Bendel on 57th street in Manhattan. The gentleman I gave it to asked, "Are you Mr. Thomasian's son?"

I answered, "Yes."

He said, "Do you know that, in all the years I've been doing business with your father, never once did we ever sign papers...his handshake was enough? You should be very proud of him."

I thanked him, shook his hand, and left. I remember so clearly the pride I felt in my heart for my father on my way back to the office. He was not a man of many words, but influenced me by example on matters of honor and hard work.

My mother, Sophie, on the other hand, would sit and talk with me about many things. She was always able to weave in messages of how a man develops his character. She was one to encourage rather than criticize. My parents taught me the important values such as honesty, honor, the value of hard work, and the love of life.

My grandmother, Zabelle Babian, was a lady, and very kind to me. She would take me by subway to Coney Island in the summer. The ride would make me sick to my stomach, and we would have to get off once or twice for it to settle down. My grandmother spoke Armenian, French, and Turkish, but very little English. She influenced my respect for elderly people.

I had a reasonable understanding and love of my country, but I'm sure, like many others of my generation, I took my freedoms for granted. After all, who was ever going to harm the United States? I did not have a burning desire to defend our freedoms. There was no need.

During the summer of 1942, I entered the Delehanty Institute to learn riveting as my part in the war effort by working in a factory building airplanes. After graduating, I got a job as a riveter with Brewster Aircraft, working on the night shift building Catalina bombers. It was quite an experience working with lot of older men. One day the union boss saw that I wasn't taking a smoking break like the others.

"Hey, why aren't you on the break?" he barked.

"I don't smoke," I explained.

He seemed upset that I wasn't going on the break. "You'd better go, or I'll never approve you when your time comes up to join the union."

I answered, "Don't you care that a war is going on? They need what we're building, so what's wrong if I'm willing to keep working?"

I finally went on the break and had a Coke, but I was amazed at this grown man's attitude. He cared more about his coffee break than putting in a little extra time riveting to help the war effort. After a few weeks I couldn't stand it any more, and I quit. I decided then to quit high school and volunteer for the air force.

My right of passage into the real world was only days away, and I spent what little time I had left with family and friends, cherishing what I thought might be our last moments together.

After I told my mother and father of my desire to volunteer for the air force, we talked it over. I explained that, if I joined now, I could choose the branch of service I wanted. I would have no choice if I waited to be drafted after graduating from high school. I told them that part of my pay could help out at home. After my parents realized my commitment, they finally gave their blessings. However, I had to promise to complete my last term of high school in the military.

My close friends, Bob Torrell, Ed Barry, and Mary Mills, were surprised but wished me well. I spent time saying goodbyes to our family and friends till the day finally came for me to report to Atlantic City for basic training.

PRIOR TRAINING

On November 6, 1942, at eighteen years of age, I enlisted in the United States Air Force. My service preference was flight training, but because my eye exams didn't meet the requirements, I was rejected. Still, my first love was the air force. I got my basic training in Atlantic City, where I stayed at the Ambassador Hotel, which had been converted to a virtual military barracks with bunks instead of beds. There were ten to twenty men to a room, or suite with two rooms. We were told to keep the place neat. At night we were to hang up our clothes in the closet. On the first night I did just that, and when I got up the next morning and dressed, I discovered that my wallet was gone. What a shock!...my introduction to the real world. After basic training, a trainload of us were sent to Airplane Mechanics School in Goldsboro, North Carolina, and from there to Electrical Specialist School at Chanute Field, Illinois. At this point, those of us with high marks were offered an opportunity to join a class in the Flight Engineers School at the Boeing plant in Seattle, Washington. We would be trained to be B-29 flight engineers by the Boeing civilian engineers. No one had ever seen or heard anything about a new bomber, but I jumped at the opportunity to be involved in something special. It sounded very exciting!

I wrote home to tell my folks what I had decided.

Chanute Field, Ill.
Friday 26, 1943
Dear Mom,

I am writing on the train going to Chicago. Boy! it's really hot. I thought we wouldn't get our passes this week, but we did. It's no fun staying in camp on one's day off.

Yesterday twenty-seven B-17's (Flying Fortresses) came to land here. Boy, they were big and beautiful. I took some pictures as they came over my barracks nice and low. It's really something to see those big things coming in to land. This morning they took off to Albany and from there overseas...all young men about 21 years old. You should have seen them take off...what a racket! They have 4 single-row R3350 engines roaring away. I'll bet it would be wonderful to have one of those planes in my charge. What destruction they can give out. They have guns all over.

I received the letter from you and Pop yesterday. Mom, I realize and can imagine how you feel about all this, and I'm grateful to you and Pop that you left the final decision up to me... for this reason. Ever since I went to A.M. School in North Carolina, I heard about this flight engineers stuff. I have been secretly wishing that I would get a chance and the honor of trying and succeeding to be one. I know perfectly well the demands are high and I'll probably be trying against boys who have gone to college and know math inside out. But I'm going to try all I can. If I don't make it, I'll at least know that I tried. The way I see it, it's an honor to be a Flight Engineer, especially on a new bomber. That's why I want it. I've always been shy of taking responsibility. Now I'll have men's lives depend on what I do. Do you think that I'd do that purely because I want to have fun? NO! this is my own personal fight to get confidence in myself so that I'll be able to take on responsibility in later life. I think that is the time a man is made, when he can tell his buddies that the plane is safe and will bring them back. Mom and Pop, if at all God wills it, I'm going to be one, and a good one too! Besides, Mom, I'm sure, in fact I'm positive that in the long run, that you'll agree with me that I took the right step. I thought real hard, Mom, believe me.

Love and kisses to you all, Karnik

Weeks later, we were shipped out by train to Seattle, Washington. When we arrived at our base next to the Boeing plant, we settled in our barracks for the night. The next morning we went to our first class in one of a number of small, fabricated attached rooms where white-smocked Boeing engineers told us that we were to learn about the new B-29. One can imagine how excited we all were. As the weeks passed into months, we were bombarded with innovations in engines, armament, pressurization of the cabin areas, and numerous other details. It was very interesting to study about a plane that one had not seen except in engineer's drawings. They had some parts of the plane in different classes, and everything looked so big and high tech. That was it until one day we all heard a roar of engines from the runway in the valley below. The Boeing plant, and their runway, were located at the bottom of this large valley with hills and mountains on all sides. Our classrooms were on a ridge several hundred feet above the valley floor. We all ran out of the classes and looked down at the two planes below...and there they were, lined up on the runway. One olive-drab B-17, and behind it was the most beautiful plane I had ever seen, a bright, shining B-29. Having warmed up their engines, the B-17 revved up and released its brakes, rolling down practically the whole runway before it took off. Now the B-29 revved up its engines till the roar was deafening, then released the brakes and lurched forward, when suddenly, using only one-third of the runway, it went straight up into the sky. Well, we let out our own roar and got back to our classes with renewed energy. Up against college boys who had a lot more math as well as engineering education, it was very difficult to comprehend the math theories. Naturally, I failed the course! I did, however, learn a lot and that knowledge helped me later in my maintenance duties as an Electrical Specialist/Gunner (1685) on our B-29. The early B-29 crews were made up of gunners who had specialties such as Electrical, Armament, and Engine. The Flight Engineer supervised them all. Later, when we formed our crews, we were lucky to have one of the best in the business...Lt. David (Burt) Parmalee.

From the Boeing plant I, along with others, was sent to Gunnery School in Denver, Colorado, to learn the special B-29 gunnery system. This was the first World War II bomber equipped with remote-control gun stations. The guns themselves were in turrets, two on the underside of the plane and two on the topside, as well as one in the tail. Each gunner had a special gun sight, on a swivel at the base of the blister window, which he had to program either before the mission or when he recognized the attacking plane. This was accomplished by inserting the appropriate wing span of the plane into the sight. Normally at the briefing of the mission, the gunner would be told the types of planes he would encounter, and he would enter the proper numbers into the system before we took off.

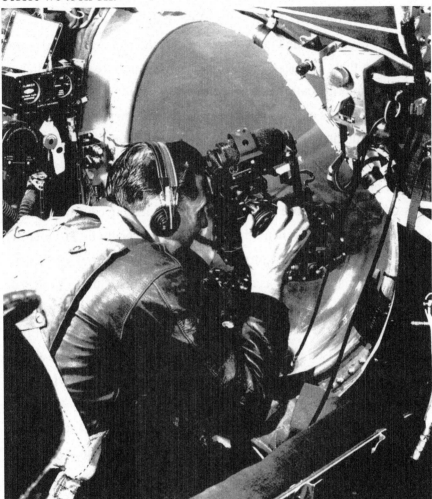

There was a flat 3 x 3" smoked sighting glass. The gunner would look into it and see orange dots arranged in a circle on the glass. These dots could be brought to the center or to the outer edges of the glass by turning the large round knobs on either side of the sight. He would see the attacking plane coming at him through this glass. He then would try to position the dots to touch the tips of the wings by turning the large knob on the sight. That would enlarge or reduce the circumference of the dots. Once the dots touched the ends of the attacking plane's wings, a trigger button would be pressed.

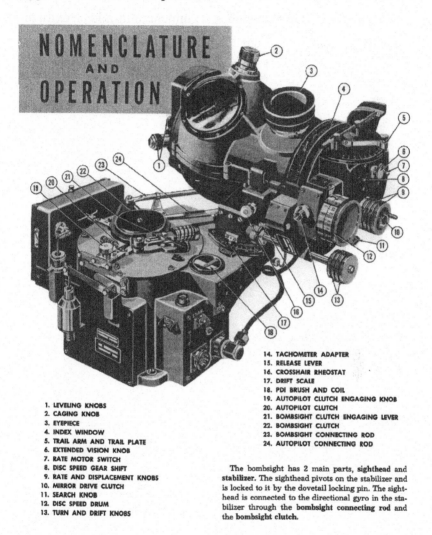

NOMENCLATURE AND OPERATION

1. LEVELING KNOBS
2. CAGING KNOB
3. EYEPIECE
4. INDEX WINDOW
5. TRAIL ARM AND TRAIL PLATE
6. EXTENDED VISION KNOB
7. RATE MOTOR SWITCH
8. DISC SPEED GEAR SHIFT
9. RATE AND DISPLACEMENT KNOBS
10. MIRROR DRIVE CLUTCH
11. SEARCH KNOB
12. DISC SPEED DRUM
13. TURN AND DRIFT KNOBS

14. TACHOMETER ADAPTER
15. RELEASE LEVER
16. CROSSHAIR RHEOSTAT
17. DRIFT SCALE
18. PDI BRUSH AND COIL
19. AUTOPILOT CLUTCH ENGAGING KNOB
20. AUTOPILOT CLUTCH
21. BOMBSIGHT CLUTCH ENGAGING LEVER
22. BOMBSIGHT CLUTCH
23. BOMBSIGHT CONNECTING ROD
24. AUTOPILOT CONNECTING ROD

The bombsight has 2 main parts, sighthead and stabilizer. The sighthead pivots on the stabilizer and is locked to it by the dovetail locking pin. The sighthead is connected to the directional gyro in the stabilizer through the bombsight connecting rod and the bombsight clutch.

In the heat of battle, if there were a few different types of planes, there was no time to identify the plane and enter the numbers into the system, so one would just follow the tracers, bullets made to release a trail of smoke or fire so that one could see where they were going and could make any adjustments in his aim. I think it was every third or fourth bullet. Another feature of this system was that the gunner could command two or three turrets to coordinate on one target from one gun sight. By flipping different switches, a gunner could add an extra turret or two onto his gun sight. I never got to use this feature in combat.

HISTORY & BACKGROUND

In preparation for the service introduction of the new B-29 bomber, the 58th Bombardment Operational Training Wing (Heavy) was activated at Smoky Hill, Kansas, and was re-designated as the 58th Bomb Wing (Very Heavy). The Wing had four groups assigned to it, the 40th, 444th, 462nd, and 468th, but it had no B-29s. The first production B-29 was accepted by the USAAF on September 21, 1943.

In November 1943, Operation Matterhorn was approved; the building of four bases in China was promised to us by Generalissimo Chiang Kai-Shek, and the British agreed to provide air bases in India. The first B-29 landed in Chakulia, India, on April 2, 1944 and by April 15 a total of thirty-two B-29s had arrived. The runways were concrete, 10 inches thick, and 7,500 feet long. Chakulia was the base of the 40th Bomb Group.

The fields in India were to be the main bases for the B-29s of the 58th Bomb Wing bombing targets from Singapore to Burma. Their operations against Japan (Operation Matterhorn) would be flown from forward airfields in China around the major city of Chengtu. There were four such fields, one for each bomb group. Wing and Bomber Command headquarters were at Kharagpur, in India; and Hsinching, in China. Bases in India were located in Bihar and Bengal provinces. All China bases were located in Szechwan province.

Unit	India Base	China Base
40th Group	Chakulia	Hsinching (A-1)
444th Group	Charra (Dudhkundi)	Kwanghan (A-3)
462nd Group	Pierdoba	Kiunglai (A-5)
468th Group	Kharagpur	Pengshan (A-7)

The fields had a single landing strip, 8,500 feet long and 19 inches thick, made of rounded rocks and gravel and covered by a native concrete, consisting of crushed rock, sand, clay, and water...and 52 hard stands. These were areas where planes could be parked and repairs made. Over 300,000 Chinese worked by hand to build the fields.

Chinese laborers, men and women, with no heavy equipment, building an airfield for the giant B-29 Superfortresses, one of four such fields in China.

On April 12, 1944, the Twentieth Air Force was activated. It was the first and only air force to be created for the purpose of taking into action a single type of aircraft...still unproven, the B-29 Superfortress. Its commander was General of the Army Henry H. Arnold, Commander of the USAAF. The B-29 Superfortress was the ultimate strategic bomber of WWII. B-29s were pressurized, had remote-control turrets with lead-computing sights, and could fly higher, farther, and faster than any other bomber, making them by far the largest and most complicated aircraft that had ever been built. They were also the first bombers that had the range and payload to take the war consistently to the Japanese homeland. It was a B-29, the Enola Gay, that expedited the Japanese surrender by dropping atomic bombs on Hiroshima and Nagasaki.

One of our B-29s flying from our base in India to our forward base in China. Flying over the "Hump" Himalayas on a clear day was a beautiful sight.

In the autobiography that follows, THEN THERE WERE SIX, I write about the Rangoon disaster as well as my POW experience. Out of eleven planes over the target, only one limped back to Chakulia, our base in India. To better establish the facts of the disaster the 40th Bomb

Group sustained on December 14, 1944, over Rangoon requires additional background.

Let me start with the matter of the *esprit de corps* of the Group. The character of any military organization is logically established by the unit's leader. The 40th had not been particularly well led. Having had four commanding officers in the three years since its founding, the Group returned to the States from Panama under the command of a West Pointer, Henry K. Mooney, who was assigned to the outfit for the purpose of bringing it home.

In early August 1944, the 40th B.G. was given over to the command of Col. William H. Blanchard, and it was during his tenure that the Rangoon disaster occurred. Blanchard was a hulking giant who had played in the line on some winning West Point football teams (he is not to be confused with the more famous "Doc" Blanchard who starred at West Point as a running back). He had risen rapidly to full colonel and had served for a short time in the Operations Office of the 58th Wing. Though short on flying experience, Blanchard was driven by strong ambition.

The lack of morale and enthusiasm in the organization born of this leadership vacuum was taken up by the body of the Group itself. The influence of those who gave the unit its leadership, personality and character were the pilots. Flying hundreds upon hundreds of hours of patrol in the Caribbean and on the Pacific side of the Zone, the Group had a nucleus of aircraft commanders with excellent flying skills and, consequently, leadership capabilities. The pilots had built up a mutual trust with their combat crews and with the ground personnel who maintained the planes, armed the guns, and loaded the bombs. Under this leadership, the men of the four squadrons in the Group had been formed into teams of fighting units.

Few, if any, of these pilots were capable of dealing in baloney—either the giving of it or the taking of it. With their lives on the line every time they took off on a mission, they dealt with a fate worse than any commander could deal out to them. The admonition "Find out who Big Brother is, know what Big Brother wants, and knuckle under" was not standard procedure among these veterans. As sure as night follows day, confrontations with Group Commander Blanchard were inevitable. At a steady rate, these pilots were rotated back to the States. It was adverse to the Group CO's design that pilots of this outspoken caliber be kept around if ways could be found to send them gracefully away.

Despite this lack of leadership created by the shortcomings of the CO, the Group performed well. It had flown 18 missions up to the time of this fateful one. It was to fly 70 combat missions, including those from India and China bases and from their base on Tinian in the Marianas. Additionally, 74 photo search and weather missions were flown.

On December 8, 1941, the United States declared war and entered World War II against the Japanese. The 20th Air Force, with General 'Hap' Arnold as Commander, formed on April 12, 1944, was comprised of the 20th Bomber Command in the China-Burma-India Theater, and the 21st Bomber Command in the Marianas.

ON TO CLOVIS, NEW MEXICO

Our crew was formed in Clovis, where we trained as a crew on B-17 bombers, because the B-29s were still in production. The members of our crew were:

Top row, left to right: Pilot; 1st. Lt. Wayne "Doc" Treimer, Co-Pilot; 1st. Lt. Chet Paul, Bombardier, Lt. James McGivern, Navigator; Lt. Norman Larsen, Flight Engineer, Lt. David "Burt" Parmalee.

Kneeling, left to right: Radio Operator, Cpl. Richard "Brooksie" Brooks; Central Fire Control/Armament, Cpl. Vernon Henning, Right Gunner/Engine Mechanic, Cpl. Leon McCutcheon; Left Gunner/ Electrical Specialist, Sgt. Karnig "Tommy" Thomasian; Tail Gunner, Cpl. August "Augie" Harmison,

(Absent:) Radar Operator, Cpl. Bob Dalton

When we had bombing practice, we all flew as a crew, but the flying was mainly for the benefit of the pilots, navigator, flight engineer, bombardier, and radio operator. The rest of us mostly went along for the ride and brushed up on our gunnery skills on the ground. Our crew had the best record for completed training flights. Some crews found ways to land at a field for minor repairs and stayed overnight. One day, we gunners thought that it would be nice to lay over in Tucson, Arizona, since our next training flight was in that direction. In order to fly in that direction from Clovis, New Mexico, we had to use oxygen to climb over the high mountains in our B-17.

It occurred to us that, if we didn't have enough oxygen to return, we would have to land at Tucson. Then we could stay over and see the town. After taking off and heading over the mountains, we opened the oxygen valves full on until we felt we had depleted them enough, and turned the valves off. We flew various mock bomb runs over Tucson and started to head back to our base. The flight engineer noticed that our oxygen was low and advised our pilot, Doc Treimer, that we should land at Tucson and check it out.

Everything was working out fine. We landed and jumped out. Doc took one look at us and absolutely blew his cool. There we were in clean suntans, smiling from ear to ear, ready to go to town. He read us the riot act, and within thirty minutes, we got our oxygen and headed home, keeping our perfect record. Rest assured, this creative ingenuity was never tried again!

Many months passed until the B-29s started rolling off the assembly line. We were most anxious to have our very own plane assigned to us. On May 30, we got our orders to go to Harrington, Kansas, where we picked up our brand-new plane. We all called home to say that we were going overseas but didn't know where. We were all charged up with the excitement of having our very own brand new B-29. Mom and Pop were always positive. I often reflected on what they must have thought.

After I got home from the war, I found out.

My mother Sophie, writing in her diary at her desk in our apartment.
She always spelled my name in the Armenian spelling ending with a 'k'.

She had written a diary for me to read.

My darling Karnik.

This diary is dedicated to you. I am writing to you almost every day, but sometimes I have to impose restrictions on my troubled thoughts. Here in the following pages, you'll see your Mom's meditations, thoughts, worried feelings, her longings for you. Her fear for your safety ...well everything. I know hard days are ahead for us, I feel it. But happiness will come to us. May God bless and save you.

Your Mom

The first entry was on July 14, 1944 with these precious words:

My precious darling:

We received notice from the war department that your address has been changed. We knew this day was coming too...It is extremely hard for your parents to have hat feeling that from now on you are quite in danger. We both try to be brave,

Karnik, but sometimes I can't help meditating why innocent people like us should be subject to endure the consequences of such atrocious conflicts.

We are quite brave, my darling, we try to hide from each other our inner thoughts and feelings....

Your last telephone was a "Goodbye". I knew it....well...."AU REVOIR" and God bless you! We all must be courageous and brave, everything will be alright, and very soon too. My darling, in 'your own' sweet way you tried to spare us from the news of your going overseas...

We flew a number of flights to familiarize ourselves with our new B-29 and also to eliminate any bugs in the systems. Our flight engineer, Burt Parmalee, was extremely good at his job. The whole crew had a lot of respect for his dedication and knowledge of all the mechanical aspects of the B-29. When he said the plane was ready, it was ready!

I remember, on one of our shakedown flights, I crawled through the tunnel from the rear pressurized compartment to the forward pressurized compartment to see how things were.

"Do you want to fly the plane, Tommy?" asked "Doc" Treimer, our pilot.

I said, "Sure."

Chet Paul, our co-pilot, got up, and I sat in his seat. Doc told me what to watch for, and to be aware of the many dials. I was doing fine until I looked ahead and saw a large bank of clouds.

"Do you want to take over?" I asked Doc.

He chuckled a bit. "You've been flying instruments all this time, so just continue."

My eyes were glued to the instruments. That's when he told me that instruments are fine, but you must learn to look about you and get a feel of what the plane is doing at the same time. The boys got a big laugh at my naivete, but I became more aware and had more respect for Doc's heavy responsibility.

July 15th

I wonder sometimes, how you feel about all this...away from home away from your country...on your way to do your duty for your Country.

Karnik darling, the memories of these days will remain forever in your young mind. You will never forget them, and when you come back, you will do everything within your power to protect and maintain the peace and liberty of your Country.

We were getting close to the time when we would get our orders to go overseas. Mr. Henning, Vernon's father, came to the base to say goodby to the crew, especially to his son and me. The three of us were walking along the wide streets of the base when Vern's father stopped, turned to us both, and, with his big hands behind each of our heads, brought us together. His deep-blue, honest, mid-western eyes pierced ours and he said to us, "Look after one another." He hugged us both and left. This moment has not left me to this day....later you will know why.

July 17th

People like us are the very essential backbone material to keep our Country's pursuit of happiness. May God be with all of us, guide us, protect us and reunite us. You are a flier now! Electrician / Gunner on the most powerful superfortress, the B-29. I am so proud of you that a boy of only 18 yrs. old, volunteered to serve your country like a grown man. Keep always your spirit high, trust in God, and BELIEVE IN HIM. Stick always to the right thing to do. God will watch over My Karnik and protect him!

July 21st evening

Indeed I received your first letter from overseas. Oh that was swell to hear again from my darling. We made several guesses as to where you are, but 'N' alone is not a sufficient key for any land to guess. New Caledonia? New Guinie? New Zealand?

July 22ⁿᵈ

Nothing much doing, I can't keep my mind away from you. Are you thinking of Pop and me too? You travel, you see many new things and new lands but for us, the folks at home, it's different. We know too well that this is not a pleasure trip for you. In war time it is also very, very hard for the folks at home too, believe me!

July 24ᵗʰ

Hurray! I have two letters from you and a package, a beautiful wooden box and a medallion. Darling, I hope and pray for you always. May your service years be light on you so you can come home safe and happy, with nothing on your mind that can bother you later on. I hope this war ends soon enough to prevent you from going into action.
I know now, you are going to India. Have faith in God darling, everything will end O.K.!

For nine months my mother could not bring herself to write in her diary.

Finally, on July 29, 1944, we received orders to go overseas with our very own B-29 . We were all in a state of high excitement. Our first stop was Morrison Field in West Palm Beach, Florida, followed by Borinquen Field, Puerto Rico. Our co-pilot, Chet Paul, said scuttlebutt had it that, if one could find a reason to land, that was the place, since there was an abundance of liquor, and it was very cheap. Chet asked the Flight Engineer if all the engines were running well. Burt said, "Yes". Chet asked him to look at the oil gauges. Burt finally got the message and suggested that we land and check out the system. We did. The officers went to pick up cases of liquor while the rest of us hung around the plane and took photos.

I remember so clearly how physically fit I felt at that time.   After the liquor was stored, we prepared to take off for Brazil.

Leon McKutcheon, Vernon Henning, Karnig Thomasian, August Harmison

We had just cleared the runway when I noticed white smoke coming from the 1 and # 2 engines, and reported it to our flight engineer over the intercom. Was my face red when he informed me that what I'd seen were vapor trails..I had never seen them before. How dumb can an airman get?

After we landed in Belem, Brazil, a leak was discovered in one of our fuel tanks. Headquarters in the States was notified to ship down a new tank. It took three weeks for the tank to arrive and be installed. Lt. Parmalee supervised the whole installation. Since we were not allowed to go to town because of the secrecy of the B-29, what else could an 11-

man crew of healthy, red-blooded Americans do but go to the beach and swim? And that's just what we did! Native women roamed the beaches selling hand embroidered table cloths. I bought one and sent it home. At last, we were ready to fly overseas.

After a fifty-five-minute systems flight check, everything tested O.K. The next morning, July 30th, we flew for twelve hours and forty-five minutes over the South Atlantic to the African Gold Coast–Accra, Ghana. We didn't stay over. The plane was checked out by Bert and the rest of us. We fueled up, ate breakfast and took off for Khartoum in the Egyptian Sudan. Eleven hours and forty-five minutes later we landed at a British airfield their. There wasn't an opportunity to see any details of the terrain because of the height at which we were flying, but the vastness of the jungle areas and the desert areas was profound.

We were forced to stay in Khartoum until the monsoons were over in India. Time passed in playing cards and watching old-time movies at night in the outdoor setup at that British base. Swimming was out of the question. The Nile, which flowed close to us, looked dirty and uninviting for a swim. The one-story concrete buildings, painted white inside and out, had been constructed by the British. Reasonably cool, the rooms were kept clean by local help. We slept on bunks with mosquito netting and ate our meals in the mess hall.

One day when we were playing cards, a young boy who helped his father with the cleaning came by and watched with great curiosity. Playfully, we asked him if he would like to join us, but he was shy. One of the guys gave him some money to play, and he said O.K.. He was enjoying himself when, suddenly, his father came by, saw his son gambling, and became extremely upset. Grabbing the kid by the neck, he pulled him away and scolded him. We told the father that his son hadn't been using his own money, but ours, just for the fun of it. He said that gambling was against their religion and forbade us to encourage this behavior in his son. The father accepted our apologies, and the incident ended. This was the beginning of my being aware of different cultures. The military never gave us any indoctrination into the various cultures we were to encounter, and I was too young to realize the importance of such information...truly a bad oversight of the military!

After nine days, the weather cleared in India:. We were given clearance to take off. I packed my things, checked our plane, and all was a GO. I was picking up the last of our bags when the little boy who'd played cards with us came by and looked at me.

"Sahib, could I come with you? I would be no trouble and would tend to your needs."

I judged him at about ten years of age. "We are going off to war, and we will not be back in America for some time," I answered. That didn't seem to deter him.

"Why do you want to come to America?" I asked.

He explained, "I know you are white skinned, but now you are dark skinned."

"Yes" I explained that I get quite dark when I am in the sun for awhile, that my skin darkens.

"Then," he responded, innocently, his enormous dark eyes welling with tears, "If I can get to America, my skin will turn white."

"No" I shook my head. "It wouldn't. But what makes you think white is better?"

"If I get to America, my skin would turn white," he insisted. His beautiful big black eyes welled with tears. What an innocent thought! What a beautiful skin color he had, and I told him so. We walked to the plane and said our goodbyes. I kneeled down on the ground and gave him a big hug, got up, and climbed aboard. To this day I can still see the little boy with his little cloth bag hanging limply from his hand as we taxied to the runway. I often wonder what happened to him.

Five hours and twenty-five minutes later, we put our wheels down in Aden, Arabia on the Gulf of Aden. Because we stayed overnight, we were able to visit Bathsheba's Baths, large, deep, cylindrical shapes lined with cut stones. The width at the top was about thirty-five feet across at ground level with stone steps going down along the inside, circling all the way to the bottom. If my memory serves me right, I would say that the depth was about forty to fifty feet.

The next morning we got clearance for takeoff to proceed to Karachi, India. It took us seven hours and forty minutes. We arrived at sundown. Burt was upset. There was a problem with the exhaust system, and we knew that to dismantle the exhaust manifolds was a real nasty job for rookies like us, but we had to do it. We were our own ground crew, with Parmalee as our chief. Thank God! He really knew what he was doing, so we got the job done in a few days.

Ever since our crew was formed, Vernon Henning and I had become close buddies. The airfield we stayed at was a commercial strip on the edge of Karachi. Vernon and I got a chance to go into the city. When we got there, we took a ride in a rickshaw, the type that was propelled with a bicycle.

I don't know who got the idea first, but we talked the driver into renting us two rickshaws. They were hesitant, but after we gave them some extra cash, they agreed and climbed onto the passenger seats as Vern and I did the peddling. Soon, we took one look at each other and took off as fast as we could down the street. The drivers were screaming at us to stop, but we kept on peddling through the people and a few cows that we maneuvered around until we were exhausted and returned to where we had started. And the drivers-- were they happy to get rid of us!

What a ride!

Parmalee had given the plane a final check; we loaded up. Finally, the tower gave us clearance to take off. Three hours and fifty minutes later, we landed at night in pouring rain at Chakulia, India. We were assigned to the 45th Bomb Squadron of the 40th Bomb Group, which was based in Chakulia. The first thirty-two B-29s and crews of our squadron had arrived in Chakulia from April 1 to 15. It had taken us six weeks, from July 30, 1944, to August 16, 1944, to fly our B-29 to Chakulia. We arrived in overcast and drizzly weather. Dreary and tired, we picked up our bedding at the supply shack. I'll never forget Leon McCutcheon's comment when he saw the big olive-drab wooden boxes against the wall. The light was dim, but we were all able to see the name, rank, and serial number, along with the words MISSING IN ACTION all stenciled in black.

Leon said, "Hey, fellas, you can get killed out here!" In our naivete we laughed, but how prophetic those words became!

MY LAST MISSION

It started very calmly in the late afternoon of December 13, 1944. Our bomb group had just received orders from the XX Bomber Command to fly its 19th mission the next day. The briefing was to be at 1930 hours. After we finished our supper, Vernon Henning, Leon McCutcheon, Richard Brooks, Bob Dalton, Augie Harmison, and I walked over to the briefing shacks, where we met the officers of our crew. Passing the line where our planes were, we noticed only two extra bomb bay tanks for this mission. Naturally we wondered where and what the target was.

Vern said, "It looks like a milkrun."

It appeared to be a simple mission, so hopefully it would be an easy milkrun. On our way to the briefing shacks, we started to make plans for a weekend in Calcutta that would surely include dinner at the Great Eastern Hotel. The Great Eastern had waiters who wore black pants and red jackets with gold buttons, and who were quick to note if a person needed water or anything else. They didn't hover around a dinner guest but were there before anyone realized that he needed something.

Finally, all our crews gathered in the large briefing room anxious to hear about where we were going and what we were going to bomb. The quiet tension was felt. Some guys did silly things, I suppose to mask their real feelings. Vern and I were sitting near the front to get a clear view, when--

"Atten..hut!"

Colonel Blanchard and his staff walked in, and the general briefing began as the adjutant uncovered the large map on the wall.

"Mission for tomorrow... Bangkok, Thailand!" The pointer moved slowly across the map

"Target...the bridge that leads to the railway yards."

We all followed the pointer as it went north to...

"Secondary target...the railway yards and station in Rangoon, Burma." Vern was right! It looked like a milkrun!

Colonel Blanchard stepped in to give us the general idea of the mission and the importance of bombing the Rama VI Railroad Bridge, which was over the Chao Phraya River. Knocking it out would stop the Japanese from re-supplying all their major units from Bangkok to Rangoon.

(Bridges, railway yards, and airfields were always our prime targets when bombing targets in Singapore, Bangkok, and Rangoon. Our targets in Japan and Manchuria were steel mills and factories.)

The Colonel left, and we all went on to specific briefings on our various specialties. We carried a mixed load of 500 and 1,000-pound bombs with no fuses...no fuses because our primary target was a bridge, and the bombs had to detonate on impact. They had small propellers that, upon release, would whirl and fall off, and the bombs would be armed. At this point, if the bombs touched anything, they would explode. It was a very dangerous load to carry, not only because the bombs didn't have fuses, but also because of the order in which they were to be stacked in the bomb bays. General LeMay always wanted a maximum bomb load over the target, and Col. Blanchard was not one to disappoint his general.

(*The following facts were common knowledge only to the lead commanders, bombardiers, and pilots at the time of the mission.*)

The ballistics for the 1,000-pound bombs were to be entered into the bombsights. The destruction of the bridge required these bombs. The Norden bomb sight could only calibrate for one weight of bomb. Since the six 500-pound composition-B bombs were loaded beneath the twelve 1,000 pounders, this meant that the 500 pounders would be released first without any precision aiming. The 500s were obviously loaded only to increase bomb tonnage.

It should be noted that the Norden Bomb Sight was a precision instrument, like a computer is today. The bombsight used the ground speed of the aircraft and a particular bomb's actual time of fall (different bomb configurations resulted in different times of fall), and combined with the autopilot of the plane to compensate for the effect of wind or drift. It was acknowledged that there was a built-in-error of 1 mil / 1,000 ft of altitude...which meant, if perfectly synchronized at 20,000 feet there would be a 20-foot error, plus or minus.

The armament officer, Capt. Frank Redler of the 44th squadron, informed his commander, Lt. Col. Ira Cornett, that "This is a bad load," and pointed out the dangers of a collision of the bombs of different weights. Lt. Col. Cornett went directly to Col. Blanchard with the facts and strongly advised him to reconsider the orders for a safe and more efficient distribution of the bomb load. Cornett pointed out the unusual characteristics of stacking 500-pound and 1,000-pound bombs one on top of the other in order to get that 'all important' maximum bomb load. He stressed the absolute distinct possibility of the bombs hitting each other after release from the racks and detonating just below the formation, causing a major explosion. But to no avail! The colonel ordered the lead bombardier to carry out the mission or face a court martial. The mission was to proceed as planned.

In our separate briefing for gunners, we were told not to expect any fighter planes and minimal if any anti-aircraft guns. It was getting to look more and more like a milkrun. With our separate briefings completed, we all headed back to our barracks for some shut-eye. We talked a bit about the mission and also about the weekend coming up and the plans we had made. Then each of us fell into our own thoughts of home, the mission, our loved ones, and slowly drifted off. Wake up was planned for 0200.

0200: We woke up, washed, packed our simple gear–khaki or fatigues, and our leather jackets, along with our .45s and a machete, which were the order of the day. No need for anything heavier, since the B-29 was the first pressurized bomber to fly in the war. We then walked to the mess hall in the dark, cool dampness of India. Vern and I always walked together wherever we went, while Brooks would go with us or tag along with McKutcheon and Harmison...it just worked out that way. Vern was one of those guys who wouldn't say a word while dressing or on the walk to the mess hall. He'd light a cigarette, and I would have a one-way conversation with him until he sat down and had his black coffee. I was used to it.

For breakfast, I had eggs sunny-side up with bacon, home fries, pancakes, and a good cup of coffee. Afterwards, we loaded our gear onto the trucks, which took us to the line where our planes were. After attending to our final check-ups, some of us stepped into the chapel for a few private words. Our navigator, Lt. Larsen, and I made our usual deal...I'd keep the fighters off the left side of the ship, and he would navigate us safely back to our base. Being part of that unusual fighting force gave us exceptional pride in our planes, ourselves, and our mission in the war. Since we were the first group of B-29s in action, there were no trained ground crews except for the crew chiefs, who really knew their stuff. Each of the gunners had a specialty, such as power-plant or armament. My specialty was as an electrical specialist. We performed as a fighting force in the air and as our own ground crew on the ground. As more trained ground crews were shipped to our base, they began to take over the main load. Our flight engineer, Lt. Bert Parmalee, had the full responsibility for the condition of the plane. He was great, the only semi-professional on our crew. Bert had worked for Pratt & Whitney before the war, designing aircraft engine parts after graduating from an engineering college. During those two weeks in Kansas, he was able to correct many of the flaws in our engines. We always considered him to be one of the reasons that we survived in India as long as we did.

0330: Take off time. Our pilot, 'Doc' Treimer, got us all together with the other officers. We gave each other pep talks, while some of us still checked last-minute things. I had just installed an auxiliary generator in the back of the ship, which had checked out fine.

After 'Doc' was satisfied that we had checked everything, he ordered, "Let's load up!"

We all climbed into our positions, and we checked our intercoms and oxygen in case of emergency. The engines were started one at a time, with the familiar high-pitched sound of the generator until the engine sputtered and then smoothed out, and soon all four engines were purring. The brakes were released, and we taxied into position with the other B-29s. It was still dark and damp from the morning dew. Looking at those big, long shapes moving slowly and haltingly along the taxi lanes, their bright landing lights casting long darts along the field as the planes were turning and stopping to get into their position in line, made my heart race. At last 'Doc' made the final turn, poised at the start of the runway with engines pulsating smoothly, ready at a signal to gather all the power that the four big engines had. It was a moment I shall never forget. The feeling was deep in my bones and in my gut. Even though it was cold and damp, I was sweating and focusing on one thing and one thing only. I knew that we had to lift off before the end of the runway. If not, with a full load of fuel and bomb bays full of bombs, there would only be vapor left of all of us. That was when I realized the value of positive thinking.

Every part of me was focused on the imminent takeoff. I unbuckled the chest strap of my chute, so I could breath easier. Vern and I looked at each other and crossed our fingers for good luck. I looked over at Leon, and we gave each other a 'thumbs up.' All four engines had been checked and revved up. Time moved so slowly. At last the throttles were pushed forward, and the plane shook with all the enormous power of the engines to hurtle us down the runway.

The sound was deafening.

Brakes were released. We lurched forward down the concrete runway, engines roaring with every bit of power the engines had to lift us, and the oblivion we had in our bomb bays, into the soft dusky sky. The concrete passed by faster and faster, and still Doc kept her on the ground. He always used as much of the runway as he could. *Whup!* We were up! Hurray! 'Doc' had done it again. What a pilot!

0800: We made our rendezvous with the rest of our formation and headed for Bangkok. Our approach to the target was covered with dense, heavy cloud cover, and the bridge could not be seen. After two bomb runs, the formation leader, Col. Cornett, ordered us to the secondary target...Rangoon railroad station and marshaling yards. It was about an hour's flight north and on the way back to our base, and I was getting itchy about having all those bombs in our bomb bays. I wanted to get rid of the load and head for home and our three-day pass to Calcutta. We knew Rangoon had only 58 anti-aircraft guns. There had been no fighters or flak up to that point in the mission.

Rangoon was soon in sight! We went directly into our bomb run at 21,000 feet. The ships were flying in an exceptionally tight formation.

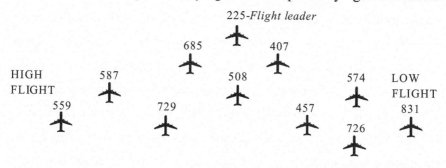

The noonday sun was beating in through the window, adding to my discomfort. I unhooked my special safety harness - a strap that went around my waist and hooked onto the floor of the plane. If the side blister ever blew out, the strap would keep me in the plane. I crawled over to the bomb bay hatch for the third time, hopefully the last, and waited for the bombs to be dropped. I had to let our bombardier know, through the intercom, that, after release, all the bombs in the rear bomb bay had fallen and none were hung up. The bombs hung in the open bomb bays poised and ready ...BOMBS AWAY!

The bays were cleared in an instant. I turned away as I called over my intercom, "All clear."

Then, suddenly, B-L-A-M!

I couldn't move. I was glued to the floor of the plane. Everything was an eerie red, as if I were looking through a red filter. The bomb bay hatch had blown open; my hand was bloody, and air was rushing all around. Moments later, I was able to move more freely, so I fully opened the swinging hatch, and saw that we were in a flat spin with flames and smoke blowing past under the bomb bays. I looked around and saw Leon turning to get out of his right gunner's seat. Vern was climbing down from his CFC (central fire control) position, and I could see that I had to get out of their way. I looked again through the bomb bay and saw what must have been a body whiz past beneath the plane, then another. Somehow, through my stupor, I was able to realize that I had to jump. None of us spoke; we must have been in shock. I doubt that we would have heard one another if we had spoken, because of the incredible rush of air coming through the bomb bay. I tried to buckle my chest buckle to my chute, but my injured left hand made that impossible. Never having jumped before, I thought that I could clasp my arms across my chest, jump, and it would be O.K. I just couldn't block the hatchway any longer. I grabbed both sides of the hatch frame, but the centrifugal force was keeping me in the ship. I gathered all the strength I could muster and finally popped out. To this day I don't remember pulling the rip cord to my chute. My next recollection was of a powerful jerk and acute strains in both my arms and shoulders. The force of the chute opening had snapped the upper part of my body out of my shoulder straps, leaving me to hang upside down. Only my leg straps were holding me from slipping out of the chute harness altogether. I was still in a daze; my actions must have been instinctive. I don't remember thinking about doing or not doing anything. I just did what I had to do automatically. No sense of emotion, or fear, or anything. I was in shock!

I grabbed my pantleg and pulled myself up enough to grab onto one of the chute straps. I kept pulling until I could get my one arm through one of the shoulder straps above me. I was right side up at last, but had to stop. My shoulders and arms were hurting, and the rarified air with all this exertion was making me so weak that I almost passed out. I tried to relax and regain my strength. It was very quiet,...only the soft rustle of my chute in the gentle wind.

"Hey, Tommy!" It was Brooks above me, yelling at me. Hearing my name brought me back to reality. I kept looking down below, praying for the last guys to jump from our spinning, blazing ship.

"Please, God, let me see more chutes," I prayed.

Moments later, there was an enormous explosion as our proud B-29 hit the ground and disappeared in a fiery burst of flame and black smoke right near our target. That was the end of "Gambler's Choice", the moniker our crew had chosen for our B-29. I was to paint it on the nose when we got back from this mission.

There were no more chutes. The realization was numbing. I knew for sure that I had lost some of my closest friends. That scene of Vern's father, when he came to see us in Kansas just before we were to go overseas, flashed before my eyes. I can never forget the look on his face.

The lower I descended, the more oxygen I was able to breathe, and my mind became clearer. It was extremely quiet...like being in another world. Bits of my life passed before me. The sound of bullets whizzing by jolted me out of my dream world. Those bastards were *shooting* at me. At that very moment, I noticed that one of the two main belts that hold the shroud lines had a 'v' cut in it about a foot above my head. That was too close, and I curled up into as small a ball as I could. Thank goodness the Japs had poor aim. As I surveyed the land below, I could see what a mess our bombs had made of the railway station. The city of Rangoon was east of the Rangoon River, and it looked like I was going to land on the west side of the river. There was a distinct difference between the east and west sides. Rangoon on the east side was a regular built-up city, while on the west side, there were lots of peasant shacks and rice paddies. My objective upon landing was to head west, towards the ocean, as fast as I could. I estimated that to be about 150 to 200 miles. If I made it to the coast, then I would head north, until I was level with an island where a radio and provisions were stored for emergencies such as this. At the time, it never occurred to me what little chance a white man would have of escaping detection in that part of the world.

The waterfront at Rangoon shows wrecked piers & sunken ships that I saw floating down in my parachute.

The ground was coming up faster and faster, and as I flexed my knees and moved my legs up and down to loosen them up.... BUMP!...I made a hard landing. Quickly getting out of the leg straps, I ripped my first aid kit off the harness and ran away from the river that I had seen coming down. Running across rice paddies, I realized that there was an army of peasants running at me from all directions. *I was a great fan of Milton Caniff, who originated and drew the comic strip,* Terry and the Pirates. *As I turned for a moment to look behind me, the scene I saw flashed me back to his strips. What a thing to think about at a time like that!* The peasants were soon all around me, brandishing knives and spears and anything else they could hold in their hands. At six feet, I towered over them. The Japanese soldiers were right behind the peasants, and they took control. I was now a prisoner of the Japanese, my life was in their hands. All my freedoms were gone in an instant.

MY LIFE AS A PRISONER OF WAR

They tied my hands behind my back, and I was searched for my .45. A Burmese peasant got it out from under my flight jacket and tried to fire it, but the safety catch was on, and he didn't know how to release it. They marched me back over the rice paddies to the river bank. When my captors pushed me around a hut, my co-pilot, Chet Paul, was sitting in the shade on the ground, leaning against the wall with his hands tied behind him. We checked each other out with our eyes to see if we were OK. So far the Japs had not roughed me up, aside from poking and prodding me to move faster. Soon, we were herded onto a little motor craft, which took us to the city on the other side of the river. While we were going across, some of the Japanese officers snapped photos of us, ...I suppose to send home. Another man, a civilian, shot some newsreel footage of us, perhaps for the six o'clock Tokyo news.

After we landed at the docks on the city side, the Japanese guards dragged us off the boat and walked us between them to a waiting truck. At that point, Chet recalls that we rode past the railroad marshaling yards, which were still smoldering. He also noticed only a few craters outside the target area. We had hit right on target. The truck stopped in front of what appeared to be a government building. We slid off the end of the truck, climbed the concrete steps to the front doors, and were pushed inside to what must have been old business offices. We stood around with our hands still tied while they figured out what to do with us. Obviously, they had not been prepared for such a situation. I saw a drinking fountain right next to where we were standing, so I quickly pressed the foot pedal and took a drink. No one stopped me.

Having finally decided, the Japanese soldiers directed us along a hallway and down a flight of stairs to what turned out to be the New Law Courts Jail, which was where we were held until our captors decided what to do with us after our interrogation. The first thing they made us do was to take off all our clothes. We were thoroughly searched and then ordered to redress. My shoulders and arms were hurting badly from my injury during the jump—the undersides of my upper arms were numb, and I felt pain when I reached above or behind during the undressing and dressing. We saw Jim McGivern and Burt Parmalee. Burt was badly injured. Something had gone clean through his biceps and broken the bone. We were able to slip in a few words, but neither man knew any more than we did about the rest of the crew, or what had become of our plane. The guards had McGivern on one side of the room, and they were laughing at him. I had noticed earlier that one of the officers had taken out his sword and cut the shoulder straps off Jim's jump suit, causing it to slip to the floor. Now we saw what the guards were laughing at. Jim had defecated in his pants. *Later we learned what had happened.* As Jim jumped out of the nose wheel hatch, he'd dived head first, and the hatch cover had slammed down on his ankle, pinning him there until the next man lifted the hatch. Chet had already jumped, along with Bert and Richard. Norm was next, and he noticed a foot caught between the hatch cover and the floor. When he lifted the hatch, the foot disappeared. Norm couldn't pull the hatch fully open because of the effect of the centrifugal force. Since he and Doc Treimer were the only ones left in the front compartment, they worked together to lift the hatch and managed to hook it in the open position. They stood there on either side of the hatch.

"It's time to go," Norm said.

Doc replied, "You first!"

Norm jumped, and that was the last time any of us saw Doc. It was a great personal loss for all of us. As it turns out, I was the only one to make it out alive from the back of the plane. All these losses hit us at about the same time. Each day we would pray that, by some miracle, the rest of the guys made it...even as prisoners. At least they would be alive. After the guards finished searching our clothing and our persons, they led us down a hall and put each of us in a cell. There was a row of big,

dark cells with bars made of 4 x 4" teak wood set three inches apart. The doors to the cells were low, about 3 ½ feet square. The cell was nine feet wide by about twelve feet deep and ten feet high. At the other end of the cell, sat a dirty white toilet with no lid. A bare light bulb hung by its wire from the middle of the ceiling. I

New Laws Court Jail

removed my shoes and crawled into my individual cell, I looked around and wondered what would happen to me.

Exhausted, I noticed a parade of spectators scrutinizing me. I soon learned that I had to stand at attention when anybody passed my cell. My mind was racing, trying to figure some sort of a plan, so that I wouldn't stumble around when questioned. When was I going to be interrogated? What would they ask me? What would they do if I didn't answer them? I was nervous but at the same time, somehow, somewhat composed. A half hour passed before the guard ordered me out of my cell, led me through a series of dark passages, and finally shoved me into a cramped room. The room was about fourteen feet square with a 3½ –foot square wooden table and two chairs.

There was one plain light bulb hanging by its wire a few feet from the middle of the ceiling. The interrogator sat down on a chair, glaring at me. He was short, squat, fat–almost bald–with eyes as cold as ice cubes. An interpreter sat on another chair, a fairly short man, wiry, with a sneering, sneaky attitude, and he spoke decent English with a smirk on his face.

"Sit on floor!"

I obeyed... and waited.

"Name?" asked the interpreter.

"Karnik Thomasian, staff sargeant, 12183215." I spelled it out as well.

"Where you come from?" he snapped . I explained that I could not tell him anything more.

"You must tell me everything!" he growled.

I repeated again that I was permitted only to divulge my name, rank, and serial number. He laughed aloud and re-issued his demands.

"What your age?" he asked.

There was no harm in that, so I believed. I told him, "Twenty."

They both smiled, and the interpreter leaned towards me, and, with a sick sneer, said, "So young to die!"

"I'm not dead yet!" I answered.

He warned me, "You will die, if you don't talk!".

The interpreter then asked me a whole battery of questions:

"How many planes were in your raid?"

"Who is the squadron leader?"

"Where come from?"

I thought I'd try to reason with them. I reminded them of the rules of war, and told them that I was given certain orders. I couldn't disobey them. I had many friends still fighting, and anything I might say could cause them to be killed.

"If you were captured," I asked, "would you talk?"

The interpreter translated all that I had said to the interrogator.

"A Japanese soldier wouldn't *be* captured. They would fight and die."

"We treat our prisoners well," I argued.

I could see that my attempts had made no impression at all. It was all a hopeless stab in the dark, and all I got was a beating with the teakwood club, which most of the guards had as part of their equipment. How naive, arrogant, frightened, and confused I was, all at the same time.

The interpreter resumed his questioning by asking me, "Would you like to see your folks again?"

"Would you like to see your sweetheart again?"

I bristled at these questions and asked them, "Wouldn't you like to see yours?"

Infuriated now, he said, "If you don't talk, you will be shot!"

At this point the interpreter picked up a teakwood club and went behind me. I kept my eyes on him, which may have saved me a fractured bone. He began hitting me about my back and arms, but I was able to ride with the blows, as I rose, dodging the blows. I still had my leather A-1 jacket on, which absorbed some of the battering from the blows.

He told me, "If you talk, I will put you in a POW camp. After the war, you can go home!"

A funny feeling came over me. I was still in a state of shock, and didn't care what he would do. I reasoned that he would kill me anyway, whether he was told anything or not. The unbelievable excitement of the day had affected me in strange ways. I had always thought of life as being very precious, but at that moment, I was willing to give it up. I had been raised to respect principles and values. The war brought me face to face with the cost of maintaining those values...the cost, my life. Why were these people fighting so fiercely, and why were they so cruel? Again, how naive I was!

The interpreter suddenly asked me, "Why are you fighting?"

I answered quickly, "My country was attacked, and I volunteered to fight and defend my country." We were fighting for the rights and freedoms of people, and I remarked that his people were trying to destroy those rights and freedoms.

The guards and interrogator snickered, angered at hearing all this. They reminded me that I would be shot, but they realized that I had made my decision. The interrogator lost his control, took off his leather sandals, and started to beat me with them. I warded off most of the blows. He went back, got his chair, quickly put it down and grabbed the teakwood club from the guard who was in the room. I quickly got up from the floor. He started swinging at me. I was scared. Again, having my leather jacket on warded off the blows.

I asked him, "Do you think this is fair? ...You can do anything you want, and I can't hit back. What kind of justice is that?"

The interpreter said, "It is all fair, since you didn't give us any information." Finally, he stopped hitting me.

I had bruises all over my body, especially my shoulders, back, and arms, but, thank God, he hadn't hit me on the head. He sat down and motioned for me to sit on the floor again. Through the interpreter, he asked an odd question. "Who do you think will win the war?"

I answered, "We will win, because God is on our side. We fight for truth, and truth will win."

They laughed heartily, "And we're right, and right will win!" I continued.

They had a great laugh at that as tears welled in my eyes. Even then, I was very emotional. I believed strongly in what I had said.

I looked up to see them gathering their papers. The guard poked me to get up, then directed me out the door and down to my cell. I breathed a sigh of relief and sat down to rest...but not for long. Apparently, the guard had been ordered to have me always stand at attention and also not to feed me. After about an hour or so, I was very tired and agonizingly thirsty. Back at our base we would have had our chow, gone to the clubhouse, and finished our plans for our weekend in Calcutta. I'm not there, I thought, I'm here, and I'd better make the best of it. I'd stand up for as long as I could, and when the guard was out of sight, I'd sit down, then get up fast when I heard him coming. This went on for a couple of hours, and still I didn't get anything to eat or drink. I asked for water, but the guards just ignored me. By then, it was well into the evening hours and very dark, except for the small light bulb hanging from the ceiling.

I was exhausted. I must have fallen asleep standing up and then just slid to the floor, because I woke up the next morning to the guard banging at the thick, teakwood bars of my cell. I quickly stood up at attention. He jabbered something that I couldn't understand, so I remained still. He finally went off down the corridor. This wasn't a dream...I really was a prisoner. Now, what was going to happen? Had they forgotten about me? I was just standing there facing the front of my cell, when a guard stopped and stared at me. He put down the bucket he was carrying and started to put a few scoops of rice from it into a tin he had brought with him. He shoved the tin through a special opening next to the door. I was so hungry that I was grateful for anything. He didn't leave any utensils, so I dug into it with my fingers. I asked for water. He must have understood me, because he came back and poured some into my tin. I was purely baffled by his changed attitude. The day before, the interrogator had said that I would be shot; today, I was fed. I couldn't understand, and I decided to sit tight and see what would happen next. Being alone in a cell gave me a lot of time to think. Christmas was just a couple of weeks away, and I prayed that my parents wouldn't be notified until after the holidays. I hoped someone had seen our chutes... what did they know about us?...who had survived, and who hadn't? I wondered if the Japs really meant to kill us. Looking around the cell walls, I noticed names and dates, and I wondered about the fate of those imprisoned before me.

Suddenly I heard a familiar voice asking the guard for something. It was my co-pilot, Chet, who had been in the next cell to my right. After the guard left, I went to the front right corner of my cell and tapped on the wall. Chet tapped back. I was so happy at that spare bit of 'conversation.' Crouching low against the bottom of the wall, we whispered through the bars. Though our voices had to carry only ten inches, we had to be very careful. I told him what had happened in the back of the plane, and he told me his story. We couldn't figure out what had happened...what had hit us. I told Chet of my interrogation the day before.

He advised, "If push comes to shove, tell them certain things that they already know, but to think before you speak."

That advice stayed with me for the rest of my internment. We stopped talking because the guard was making his rounds again. Close to the noon hour, another prisoner was put into my cell. I had never seen him before, but he had a 20th Air Force patch on his sleeve. His name was Stanley Dow.

Was this a plant? Were the Japs trying to get information out of me? I decided not to talk to him.

That afternoon I contacted Chet again

"Tommy, our plane wasn't the only one which went down. Another 20th Air Force man, named Edward Trinkner, was put in my cell."

I told Dow of my conversation. He said, "Ed is my tail gunner." Slowly, I started to trust him. Dow told me his story about taking the place of one of the regular crew members on this mission. What a bad break! Now, the big question was, what was going to happen to us?

Soon, more rice was doled out with a mix of vegetables. I ripped off my leather C.B.I. patch from my jacket and used it as a scoop with which to eat. It was good to have some food again. After eating, we talked a bit when the guards left. I guess we were all on edge. Something had to happen soon.

After nightfall, something did. The guards batted their gun butts on the wooden bars and ordered us out of our cells. We crawled past the small door of the cell, quickly putting on our shoes. The guards ordered us along a hallway, which led to a small, open, dark courtyard. It was about fifteen feet by twenty-four, with a hard dirt ground. That's when I saw Richard Brooks, my radio operator, for the first time. He was alive, appeared to be well, but his face looked very worn. I could see that he was frightened. I looked around, and all I saw were Japanese officers with their swords. We were ordered to kneel down in a row and remain silent. My mind really started to race over all the possibilities. Was this the way it would end? I just couldn't believe the scene. The door we came through opened again, and I recognized more of my crew joining us. There were now only six of us! I was relieved and so happy to see Norman, my navigator. We winked at each other as he knelt down beside me. Parmalee was suffering with his broken right arm. Later we learned that his right arm had been broken when bomb fragments from the explosion of the bombs hit our plane. He needed medical attention, but at that moment that was not uppermost in our minds. A large Japanese soldier, bare chested, entered the courtyard and walked around waving his sword over his head, as if in some bizarre exercise that preceded a beheading, as if he were exercising. What now?

The guards ordered us to place our hands behind our backs as they handcuffed us all together. They came around in front of us. The chief officer held out a sheet of paper and began reading in Japanese. Was this our notice of execution?

The interpreter translated the message to us. I was stunned!

He told us, "You are to be transferred to a prisoner of war camp!"

The guards all laughed, knowing full well that we assumed we were to be beheaded. That was why they were waving their swords around.

I nearly passed out realizing that. We were led out onto the street, to an old flat-bed truck. Piled into the back, we were warned not to try to escape or to talk to each other. Two guards stood on the back of the truck with their rifles cocked. The night was cool; it was a slow, eerie ride through the poorly lit streets. Because there was no cover to the back of the truck, we could look out and see all the bombed buildings. Actually we could look right through the concrete skeletons up to the moonlit skies. This was the first I'd ever seen of the destruction of our bombs had inflicted. Awesome!

After a short ride, we reached our destination. The guards got off and motioned us to follow. We helped Parmalee off as gently as we could. Among the men of the other crews in the truck with us was one in great pain. His wrist and hand were hanging from his arm. Later, we found out that he was M/Sgt. Richard Montgomery of Capt. Meyer's crew. The Japanese couldn't, or wouldn't, do anything for him.

The massive teakwood doors of the prison opened, and we filed in. The doors were shut behind us, and we were ordered to sit down. The area was twenty feet wide, thirty feet long, and twenty-two feet high, with an arched ceiling. A number of candles along the concrete walls

Main entrance to Rangoon Central Prison.

threw off the only light, aside from the candles on the wooden table behind a translucent makeshift screen. Some of us were still standing, so we were forcefully ordered to sit on the floor and not to talk. Sitting at the table was the commanding officer of the prison. Beyond that room, and into the interior of the prison, was a menacing darkness.

We were all looking around trying to see if we could recognize anyone. The C.O. called the first man, Lt. Lionel Coffin, co-pilot on Captain Meyer's crew. He was ordered to sign a paper before entering the prison, stating that he would not try to escape. If he were caught trying to...he would be shot. The tenseness in the air was rife with anxiety. He refused to sign, stating that he was an officer of the United States Air Force and was sworn to follow orders. Since he had been ordered not to sign any papers, he could not sign this one. The guards promptly started to hit him. Still, he refused to sign. The other guards walked among the rest of us and bashed us over our heads and backs, giving us all a very clear message. This was to be one of many scenes which would forever be etched in my memory. The guards finally gave up on Coffin for the moment and ordered other men to the table. Eventually everyone signed the paper except Coffin. I pondered about what I should do. If I didn't sign, I would get beaten up like Coffin. If I did sign, what would it all mean? If I found a way to escape, I would, whether I had signed or not. In either case, if I were caught escaping, I would be shot. I signed!

All the prisoners were led into one of the buildings in this old British prison. The prison had a small central building and a number of other long buildings jutting out from the center, much like the spokes on a wagon wheel. After we were directed to our cells by twos, threes and fours, we were all given our prison numbers. Mine was #1119. Our crew was ordered to the second floor. Norman, Bert, Richard, and I were put into one cell with a dirty old burlap bag for each of us. All the gates were locked, and the guards left. Some of the prisoners, who saw us come in, knew the guards would not be back that night, and they started to ask questions and gave us some quick advice. One of the things we found out was that the building we were in was for solitary confinement, Compound #5. Only airmen were placed there. We looked out of the small barred opening, a foot and a half by two, at the end of the small cell and saw the stars in the dark sky above.

Japanese hated the American airmen, and we were reminded of that whenever the guards would just walk in, pull a guy out, and beat him up for no reason at all. Normally, there would be only one prisoner in a cell, but it was getting crowded, so more prisoners were placed in a cell as needed.

We were all physically and emotionally exhausted, but we related our

Aerial view of Rangoon Central Jail. Going clockwise from Compound #1 with the words 'JAPS GONE' on the roof. This compound housed the Chinese prisoners. Compounds 2 & 3 mostly British, #4 was bombed out. Compound #5, solitary was a smaller one and just a piece of the roof can be seen. Compounds #6 & 7 housed mainly British, Aussies, New Zealanders and some Americans. All airmen from compound #5 were moved to Compound #8 when the Japanese realized that the British were heading south from Mandalay to liberate Rangoon.

individual experiences to each other in the darkness of our surroundings. Despite the moans of some of the wounded men, we fell asleep.

December 18, 1944. We woke up early to a noisy compound from guard activity. One came around to all the cells and took a long hard look at all of us. After he left, the regular guards took over. There were two, one for downstairs and one for upstairs. It was about 7:00 a.m.

when we got something to eat–more rice, and some brown stuff that didn't look so appetizing. We tried it, but it tasted awful, and we couldn't eat it. After the guards had left the building for a short while, the older prisoners gave us some valuable advice. They made a big point about the brown stuff. They called it "nucca," It was the brown shells of the rice that were ground up and boiled in water. Since it was the only source of Vitamin B in the prison, we had to eat it. The veteran prisoners made it clear that if we didn't, we would get beri-beri for sure, a disease of the nerves resulting in partial paralysis, swelling of the legs caused by the abnormal accumulation of body water or serous fluid. Eventually, one could die from this without proper treatment. That was enough for me. I found out that if I ate it right away while it was still warm, I could get it down. After a time, I didn't notice the taste and never missed another scoop.

Our cell was six feet by twelve, with about a ten-foot ceiling. The window had no glass, just bars. The whole cell was made of concrete except for the iron bars. We started to look out the window to observe more of the prison complex. Because of the walls between the various compounds, we were not able to see much. However, we were able to see windows similar to ours on the second floor, which turned out to be compound #6. Soon, we noticed men waving and using sign language. We took turns answering and having, what you could, under these circumstances, call a conversation. It was the beginning of many such

Cell in solitary cellblock #5, Rangoon Central Prison where all Air Force POW's were kept.

conversations.

Time to take out our Binjo box–a used ammunition box, which served as our toilet! The routine was that every mid-morning one person in each cell would carry it out at the command of the guard and pour it into a trough along side the building. At the same time he would grab as many leaves as he could from the trees surrounding the trough for the men in his cell to be used as toilet paper. It was our only opportunity to leave the cell and get a breath of air. The guards were always rushing us, but it was a cherished few moments. It was on this first day that I noticed some of the other prisoners in the other cells. I looked cautiously into each cell I passed, careful not to spill anything from my Binjo box. Constant starvation had left its mark on wasted, thin bodies and pale, drawn, gaunt faces. Our bunch, recently imprisoned, could easily be spotted as different from the others just by their complexions and the condition of their clothing. The veteran prisoners were covered with scabies and jungle sores. There were a few with beri-beri, and others who were just lying down in their cells waiting to die. It scared me to think that in time I could be like that.

About noon on that first day, the guards came to our cells and told us to put on whatever clothes we had and stand just outside our cells. So far there were about ten to twelve of us who had been captured on our raid. Gathering us together, the guards took us downstairs and out into the open ground bordering the building. We wondered what was coming next. One of the officers explained that pictures were going to be taken of us. It seemed that we had passed our propaganda screen test. Pictures were taken, and we were ordered back into our cells.

About six that evening, we got our second meal of the day, rice and just a sparse mix of vegetables. That was it for that day and every day after that. At the end of each day, the guards counted all the prisoners, locked the cell block doors, and left us alone for the night. That's when all the whispering started. The old prisoners gave us more advice and helped us with some useful Japanese words and commands. They told us what the guards expected of us, and how we had to bow when they came by our cells. We should never be caught sitting down or they would beat us. All this information was a great help. It probably saved us many a beating. Then we answered questions from the hungry minds of the older prisoners for news of the outside. Where were we from...the latest from the home front, especially in this theater of war? They even wanted to know the latest song hits.

One of our men sang a couple of them, which the others loved and appreciated. Then Lionel Coffin, who was on the ground floor, asked us to remain quiet so that he could read to us from the Bible. Somehow, he had managed to smuggle one in, and, every night, he would read from it. This was a very emotional moment. No place of worship, however large, however adorned with statues of gold, could ever capture the genuine purity of this religious experience. Each night, it gave us hope and assurance that one day we would be released from this nightmare and go home. After the reading, we were led in prayer and all joined in the Lord's Prayer. Our first full day in solitary was at an end.

The next day started like the first, with the noisy guards hitting the iron bars on the cell doors. We were stiff from sleeping on the hard concrete. What we wouldn't have given for the thinnest of GI blankets! The discarded burlap rice bags were of little value. Soon the rice and nucca were served by a small Chinese prisoner with friendly eyes. He was the same man who gave each of us a beat-up, six-by-eight-inch galvanized tin and doled out the rice and nucca. He always had a small black skull cap on his head with a full white shirt and black, loose fitting pants that came just below his knees. He wore leather sandals, which made a patter of soft steps as he approached us. We became conscious of every type and patter of sound. It was hard to tell how old he was, but

I thought in his late twenties. Whenever I saw him, he had a gentle manner about him. There was always a guard hovering over him, so he couldn't speak to us or give us anything underhanded. Apparently, we were not going to get any utensils, so I kept using my leather CBI patch.

In the daytime, we 'talked' from one compound to another. In the evenings, after the guards had left, we talked from one cell to another. Every day we learned more about the prison and the way we were to live...how to act with the guards...why we were in solitary as opposed to other prisoners in the other compounds. I found out that the air force men were singled out to be in solitary, because we were 'indiscriminate bombers.' and the Japs wanted us to pay for the Doolittle raid. Therefore, we were not allowed any extra privileges such as living in a regular compound where we could walk around and talk to the other men, or go on work details and get "better" food rations.

We tried to pass the day as best we could with word games, such as naming all the states in alphabetical order, each man taking his turn. Then we would switch to dogs or birds or any mental-type game. At mid- morning the little Jap we had encountered when we first walked into the prison came and stood in front of our cell. He looked at the nameplate on the outside of our cell.

"Tomasan?"

I answered,"Heit!" The equivalent to "yes". He unlocked the gate, led me downstairs and outside, to a small shack near the right front of our compound. He hadn't asked me to take all of my clothes with me, so I figured this couldn't be too much to worry about. I entered the shack and saw two Japanese sitting at a small wooden table. I remembered seeing one of them when they were taking pictures of us just outside this shack. The interrogating officer wore a pair of glasses with thick light-blue lenses over a pair of cold, penetrating eyes. He told me to sit in the chair opposite him while the other Japanese–a civilian–sat to one side of the table. The interrogator could speak a little English. He started to ask me a lot of the same questions that had been asked of me at the New Laws Court. We exchanged many words in the next half hour.

"What is your home address?" he demanded.

"Why do you want to know?" I asked.

"It is to tell your parents that you are O.K."

I told him, "You can send my serial number and my name to my government, and they will notify my parents. That is the regular procedure." He wouldn't listen.

I said, "I believe that you plan to harm my folks."

He blustered, fumed, and finally blew up when I wouldn't tell him anything about the B-29 or other details. The interrogator got up, picked up his rawhide whip, and started slashing at me. It was only two feet long but it hurt. Trying to stand, I fended off the blows with my arms. A guard added to the brutality by belting me with a teakwood club, which all the guards seemed to have.

"I can't tell you anything!" I repeated.

Finally, he stopped. Sitting down I tried to think of what to do next. Suddenly, I remembered what Chet had told me back in the New Laws Court lockup: "Make up plausible answers, which they probably know already, without compromising valuable information."

The interrogator asked me more questions and placed a sheet in front of me with a list of questions. I thought, let me act as if I'm cooperating. I started to answer the questions approximating our air speed, range, bomb load, armament, and maximum altitude. I gave him numbers that were far from correct. I told him, "I don't know the answers to all the questions." He believed me.

When the interrogation ended, I was put into a cell by myself. No doubt it was to keep me from telling the others what I'd said or hadn't said. I was totally alone for the next couple of hours, when suddenly the door opened and Parmalee was shoved into my cell. He had been beaten even though he was badly wounded.

"Burt? Were you beaten much?" I asked.

He said, "When I couldn't answer some questions, they slapped me around, but they soon realized that I was too weak to continue with the interrogation."

There wasn't much I could do to comfort him. I told him what I'd gone through, and we spent the rest of the day in this cell trying to cope with our pain and anxiety.

When we were put in our original cell with Norman and Richard the next day, we breathed a sigh of relief. Naturally, our buddies wanted to know what happened to us. "Did they beat you?"–"What were their questions?"–"What did you say?"

We talked the rest of the day about how to handle ourselves in these situations. When we got right down to it, there wasn't much we could control.

The next few days were more or less uneventful, until a guard came by and called my name.

"Tomasan!" He unlocked the door and motioned for me to come out. I wondered what was going to happen now.

"See you later, guys," I said casually.

The guard pushed me ahead of him down the stairs and out the front gate, then turned towards the little interrogation shack.

Here we go again, I thought. I stood outside until they got good and ready; then the guard pushed me inside. I was told to sit down in the same old wooden chair. This time there was a new cast of characters. Right across from me was an East Indian in some sort of officer's clothes with sashes and braids all over him. I later found out that he was Capt. Chandra Bose, a high ranking officer of the Indian National Army, which was strongly and very actively anti-British. He had an aide with him who took down everything in writing. Capt. Bose wore a turban, signifying he was a Sikh. On my left was a Japanese naval officer who didn't have much to say. I suppose he was there to satisfy his curiosity.

Capt. Bose spoke English with a British accent.

"Have you ever heard of Ghandi?" he queried.

"Yes, I've heard of him."

He suddenly got angry. "Why have the British imprisoned Ghandi?"

Looking at him, I said, "As far as I know, Ghandi wasn't in prison. Somebody is fooling you."

"I am going to ask you questions about your base in India. "Don't lie," he said arrogantly, "because if you do, I will know. I have my men all over India."

"Well," I said, "if that is so, why ask me? Why not just ask your men?" I didn't think that was the most tactful thing to say, but it was already out.

He said. "You are very arrogant, and it would be better for you to answer my questions. Here is a sheet of paper and pencil. Draw a diagram of your airfield in India."

"No, I won't!" I answered, but that didn't get me very far. I sat and thought for a moment and decided to do what he asked, but in as generalized and deceptive a manner as possible. I was pretty good at drawing, so I could make it look believable. Picking up the pencil, I drew a runway, then a road horizontal to it going quite a distance. Along the road I put a post exchange building, some tennis courts, a large area for a baseball diamond, and an N.C.O. clubhouse. The Indian and the Japanese became irritated.

"Where are the *hangars*? "Where are the *planes*?" they wanted to know.

I scattered a few hangars around, and I said that there were about sixteen to eighteen planes scattered all around, and not in one place.

They didn't seem to question the validity of all the mock buildings I had drawn.

"What about the other fields?" they countered.

"I never saw any of them," I responded, "because I had just arrived in India, and I'm unfamiliar with other bases."

Capt. Bose continued his interrogation. "Where did you go on your passes?"

I told him, "I wasn't there long enough to get a pass."

"You must have gone to Kharagpur, which was so close." I figured that I would tell him I had gone there, since the men from all the fields go there. I wouldn't give him any info about the field from which I'd come.

He asked me, "What did you do there?"

I told him, "I usually got some ice cream or saw a movie at the British-American U.S.O. with some of the men."

He asked, "Do you like ice cream? Would you like some?"

I said, "Sure, do you have any?"

He yelled, "You wise guy, eh?" The guard batted me around and practically threw me out of there, but not before I was made to bow. I was relieved to get back and see my buddies again.

A few days later the guard came and took Burt Parmalee with him, maybe to be questioned. Some time passed before the guard came back and took me out of the cell and directly to the interrogation shack. I saw Parmalee in the same wooden chair in which I had been sitting, and across the table from him the same Japanese interrogator with the blue-tinted glasses who had questioned me on our first day in the compound. Parmalee had a sheet of paper in front of him with the same questions they had given to me. He did not look too good. This was getting a bit complicated. If his answers were far different from mine, one or both of us would be in for a beating.

The interrogator pointed his finger at me and said, "You write his answers on paper. I sat down next to him and could see that they had beaten him even though he had a broken arm with an exposed wound. This was not going to be easy; they were watching us carefully.

We got ready to start answering the questions. I had one advantage – I was writing, and I could put down whatever I wanted. Burt read the questions and gave me his answers in a very weak voice. I put the figures as close to mine as I possibly dared. Since mine were all approximations, we couldn't possibly have the same numbers. The interrogator didn't like this low talking, but, possibly because of Burt's condition, we somehow squeaked through the interrogation to our captors' satisfaction. After we finished, he looked over the sheet and called the guard to take us back. I had to help him, especially going up the stairs to our cell. The guard opened our cell door, and Norman and Richard helped me lay Burt down onto the concrete floor. The cell door was locked, and the guard left.

We told Richard and Norman what had happened, what had been said, and about the beatings poor Burt had endured. By this time, we all had bruises and black-and-blue marks on our bodies. We had survived another day.

The kind Chinese prisoner came with the guard as usual. We would slide our tins under the bars, and he'd plop in the rice and pour the tea in our cups. They would leave, and we would eat and talk quietly about our situation, and then go to the window and try to signal the guys in compound #6. After some exchanges we would wave good-bye and sit and talk until we slept.

The next day, we heard more about Capt. C. C. Meyer's crew. We got this information in bits and pieces over the next week, mostly at night, when the guards had left. Meyer's crew was part of our ill-fated formation. Heavily damaged as a result of our bombs colliding as they were released from the planes, their aircraft was kept under control by the Grace of God and the flying skills of Capt. Meyer and the co-pilot, Lt. Coffin, until all hands had bailed out.

M/SGT Richard Montgomery (Monty),who had suffered a serious injury to his left hand, was their Radio Operator. Except for an inch of flesh, his left hand had been severed at the wrist by bomb fragments. Grasping his left wrist with his right hand, he'd been able to stop the bleeding, letting go long enough to pull the rip cord. After landing in a dried-up rice paddy, he was quickly captured by a group of irate Burmese, one of whom tried to shoot him with his own pistol. Fortunately, Monty never kept a round in the chamber, and the Burmese didn't know how to cock the pistol. After several unsuccessful attempts at firing it, the other Burmese took him to a nearby village. Monty succeeded in getting one of them to tie a tourniquet around his wrist. He was led into a small bamboo building and permitted to lie down on a table. Quickly, he gave himself a shot of morphine from his survival vest. Just then, members of his crew, Joe Levine, Bombardier, and Marion Burke, Navigator, were prodded into the room, where they saw Monty on the table. They were not injured but were very concerned about him. Joe quickly removed some sulfur powder from his survival kit.

"Monty, I'll sprinkle some of this on your wound," he offered. He then improvised a sling for the arm, using a piece of board and a length of parachute cord, and gave him another shot of morphine.

A short time later, several Japanese soldiers arrived and took all the airmen into custody. Transported by truck and river boat, they arrived at a Japanese army post for interrogation. At regular intervals, all during their journey, Joe Levine would loosen Monty's tourniquet and then tighten it again in an effort to avoid gangrene. Along the way, they were joined by Bill Walsh, their flight engineer, and Bob Derrington, a pilot observer, on his first mission.

Lt. Derrington had just arrived in Chakulia a day before the mission. The commanding officer told him that this would be a good opportunity to go along as an observer to get an idea of what a mission feels like, especially since it was a "milk run." Some "milk run!"

While the others were interrogated, Monty was taken to a flimsy field hospital where the orderlies severed his hand from the remaining piece of flesh, sewed up the stump, and bandaged it. By this time (probably ten to twelve hours after the mission), his wound looked gruesome. The orderlies didn't even bother to wash their hands, so Monty knew that infection was inevitable. By then, it was daybreak, and the crew was loaded onto a truck and driven to the Rangoon POW Prison. After entering the gates, the five men were lined up and a guard went down the line, slapping each prisoner in the face! They were then taken to the second floor of Cell Block #5 and put into a small cell with a wooden platform on which to sleep...no bedding...and an empty, leaky ammunition box for a Binjo box.

Every other day, an orderly would come into the cell, undo the dirty bandage, look at Monty's stump, shake his head, and depart. Gangrene had set in.

One morning he appeared and announced, "Today...amputation!"

He then led Monty downstairs to the pump house, a small corrugated building where the prison well was located. A Japanese warrant officer, and the prison medical officer, were waiting. It was later learned that he wasn't even a doctor. Though he spoke no English, the medic had no trouble communicating his contempt of Monty. He injected a syringe of what Monty assumed to be a local anesthetic into his shoulder. Whatever it was, he apparently injected it into the wrong place, because instead of numbing his arm, it affected his breathing. He pinched

Monty's arm with tweezers to see if he could feel it. When he winced with pain, the medical officer became angry. He tried again with the same results. Growing frustrated, he slapped Monty in the face a few times and ordered him back to his cell. He was sure the Japs would have no more concern for him and would just let him die. Three or four days later, the little Jap orderly came into his cell and again announced,

"Today...amputation!" and made a cutting motion with his right hand across his left forearm.

Monty was not overjoyed at the prospect of going through the same ordeal again. He indicated his unwillingness to cooperate.

The orderly said, "No-no! Today, good doctor–English doctor!"

We had been informed, through hand signals at the cell window, that there was a real doctor in the British compound. Now, Monty was filled with hope. His prayers had been answered. They walked to the same building.

Gathered inside were the prison commander and several of his officers, including the warrant officer, who had botched the first attempt. There were also two British POWs, an older man in his late fifties and a younger man of, perhaps, thirty. Monty was shocked at their appearance. Each wore nothing but dirty loin clothes; their bodies were covered with scabies, and their legs were swollen from beri-beri. These men had been POWs for over four years, since the fall of Burma to the Japanese.

The older man introduced himself "I'm Colonel MacKenzie."

We later learned that he was a Scotsman–an admirable man who had the opportunity to be flown out of Burma with the rest of the high-ranking officers with their medical officers when the Japanese overran Burma. Instead, he chose to be captured with the troops so that he could help with their medical problems.

The colonel explained, "Monty, I'm going to amputate the arm, and the only anesthesia available is one syringe of novocaine. There will be a great deal of pain, but with God's help and that of my assistant, Lt. Ramsey (the younger POW, also a doctor), you'll get through it as well as can be expected."

Col. MacKenzie noted there were few instruments at his disposal... nothing to cut through the bone. He would have to sever the arm at the elbow joint. In a hospital, he would have been able to cut lower on the forearm, so that Monty would have the use of his elbow joint. The Colonel also pointed out that in the prison environment, there would be no post-surgical care, and that an open bone would require dressing and medication daily.

Monty lay down on the iron army cot, and the Japs arranged themselves on chairs in a semicircle around it to watch the show. After injecting the novocaine, and with Ramsey holding Monty down, Col. MacKenzie began to cut. The amount of anaesthetic was woefully inadequate for that type of surgery. Monty screamed in pain. This irritated the Jap warrant officer, who left his seat and approached Monty with his hand raised, as if to strike him, but changed his mind and swore instead. Col. MacKenzie proceeded with the amputation. Monty continued to scream with each new cut. We could hear him from our cells, but there was nothing we could do. Eventually, the arm was amputated at the elbow and stitched. The show was over, and the Japs left. Monty's cell mates, Joe Levine and Bill Walsh, were allowed to come and help him walk back to his cell on the second floor. All of us who saw and heard Monty's screams could not believe that a man would be put through such an ordeal and then be forced to walk back to his cell with the aid of his buddies. The inhumanity of the Japanese was clearly evident from the beginning of our imprisonment to the end. Two or three days later, the little Jap orderly came in and painted the stump with

Mercurochrome, but provided no clean bandage. Monty worried about infection. In spite of the unsanitary conditions, miraculously his wound began to heal.

Days passed with more interrogations. One day stands out vividly in my mind as one of the most idiotic encounters with the Japanese mindset. Always unpredictable, it was hard to understand the Japanese soldiers' motives for doing some things, especially during these interrogations. I was sitting in the familiar wooden chair opposite the surly interrogator with the blue-tinted glasses. He had been impressed by my ability to draw in our previous session.

"Draw a B-29 with all its armament!" he ordered.

"That's impossible." I told him.

Fortunately I had worn my leather flight jacket, because I was immediately battered about my back and shoulders. Finally, after the beatings stopped, a paper and pencil were shoved in front of me again. Chet's earlier advice came to mind. I started to think fast. I drew the silhouette of the B-29, and began placing 50-caliber machine guns and 20mm cannons all over the plane. I was either going to get away with it or have my head handed to me. When I completed the drawing, it looked mighty impressive. I wish that I had it with me now.

"Ah-so...very good, do," said the interpreter. Apparently, they'd liked it, too. I was sent back to my cell immediately. Still very concerned, I didn't know why they hadn't gone to one of the crashed planes to take a look. It was beyond my belief that the fire had been so destructive, to the point of melting all trace of armaments. But such was the mindset of those Japanese at that time.

During the following days, the guards kept us on edge with their beatings. One day, we were standing around in our cell waiting for one to appear. He was very drunk. We snapped to attention and bowed, as always. For some reason, he didn't like something about Richard.

Maybe his fingers weren't placed straight and rigid at his side. Whatever the reason, he unlocked our cell door, came in, and started beating Richard with his teakwood club, as if he were swinging at a baseball. How and why he didn't turn on the rest of us is still a wonder. Luckily, Richard was trying on my leather jacket before the guard came, or he would surely have had some broken bones. If any of us had intervened, it would have been the end. We were convinced, after many such beatings, that these must have been the dregs of the Japanese army...they were animals. History has shown that even our forces were not immune from having such types. This sort of situation occurred every day...some better, some worse.

After a few days they brought in what proved to be the rest of our captured group. We still had no idea how many planes had gone down. This last addition to our numbers made it twenty nine men from our mission. Eighteen had either died from the explosion or were not able to get out of their planes. *(After we were liberated, we heard that 1ˢᵗ Lt. Hallouran Soules of B-29 #225, the only plane to make it back to our base, died from wounds he had received over Rangoon.)* Five died from our crew alone. All the men on Captain Gerber's crew died when their plane #726 disintegrated in the explosion over the target. I was very surprised to see one of the tail gunners who had flown with us on our previous missions. Augie Harmison had been in the hospital with some kind of fever of unknown origin. He had just been released for combat duty, so he came with us. I recall how upset this other gunner was when I told him that Augie had been killed. After all, if Augie had not been well enough to go, then this fellow would have been in Augie's shoes.

Christmas and New Year's Eve! Suddenly, the holiday season was upon us. What a place to spend it! Upon reflection, we were grateful that we were able to spend it at all, wherever that might be. With all my concentration on the coming holiday season, it is not surprising that while sleeping I had a wonderful dream. I was home with the family, enjoying everyone's company. Mom was cooking, and my dad and I were playing backgammon. My grandmother was hovering over me, kidding me about my moves. Pretty soon we were eating at the table and having a real good time......

"What is that noise? Who's tugging at my *arm*?"...

"WAKE UP! The guard's coming."

I don't think words could describe my utter surprise, confusion, disbelief, and total despair, all in a matter of seconds. The reality hit me like an avalanche. I stood up fast and snapped to attention just as the guard passed our cell. Another day had started in this God-forsaken place, but I am alive, I thought, and I will survive!

On Christmas Eve, the Japanese CO came to our compound and gave all four of us cigar-shaped things. The guys called them cheroots. He said they were his present, but we later found out that the other compounds had chipped in from their rations enough to give us all a treat. We thanked them, in that brief period just before sunset, when we got a chance to 'talk' to them with sign language. With the guards gone for the night and the darkness falling, a voice quite unexpectedly filled the solitary compound. It was Jack McCloskey, an American prisoner on the first floor, who sang in his Irish tenor voice, "White Christmas," and followed it with "Silent Night." Lionel Coffin said a prayer that evening, and we sang until the guard touring the outer wall growled, "KRAA!", (Loosely translated, it means "shut-up"). That was all we could do that night. However, we could hear the other compounds still singing. We could see a wisp of sky through the barred window, stars twinkling, and the moon shining brightly. The memories of our families and loved ones drew our thoughts inward. I wondered if my parents were looking at the same moon. If only I could tell them that I was alive, and that I would survive and come home! How many more times will it shine on me in this wretched place? My first Christmas as a POW. How many more would there be?

Wally Trigwell, an Australian RAF pilot, recalls that night vividly, since he had only just arrived in our compound that evening.

He says, "I was talking to my cell mate when I heard someone singing solo. Being an Aussie who had seen only one white Christmas, I was moved by the rendition of "Silent Night." Peering through the floor grating outside my cell almost opposite and below on the first floor, I saw the American POW, Jack, covered with only a little loincloth, ribs so prominently showing but singing with all the feeling anyone could have mustered. Until this day, when I hear that carol being sung, the vision of Jack McCloskey comes to mind immediately."

The rest of the week passed like all the other days, with occasional, senseless beatings and more interrogations for some of the men. New Year's Eve was upon us. We drifted into our memories and finally fell asleep on the concrete floors.

New Year's Day meant nothing to the Japanese. For them it was just another day of beating us for their entertainment. In the afternoon, news was received that B-29s had raided Tokyo. The guards were filled with hatred. One guard on duty, whom we had dubbed "Tarzan," was extremely mean and ruthless. We were in for it, and we knew it. We kept on our toes, doing our best bowing with arms straight at our sides and hands flat against our thighs, bowing from our waist with a straight back. We looked straight ahead and bowed without making any eye contact. "Tarzan" was satisfied. Of all the cells that had B-29 men in them, ours was the only one he didn't enter. It was truly a miracle.

I saw him take one man out of his cell and beat him mercilessly. He was a lefty, and he reminded me of the baseball player Mel Ott as he lifted his leading leg and swung with his teakwood stick, hitting the poor man over and over as he screamed in pain. How he didn't kill the man,

I'll never know. More beatings went on, down the walkway out of our sight, but we could hear the blows hitting the men as they fell moaning to the concrete floor. After he left, we were drained and shaking from the strain of the last hour. What a way to spend New Year's Day. That evening we were left alone and given strict orders that we were not to sing or talk. We sat at our windows and gazed at the stars. The sky is very beautiful in that part of the world. At night, the stars can be seen very clearly. Looking past the bars of our windows and gazing up at them, all of us were lost in our private dreams. Maybe our loved ones were looking at the same stars...what fantasies filled our minds. Just then we heard wonderful sounds from the #6 compound next to us. The Brits were allowed to sing, and sing they did. Little Irish ditties, American songs– "Auld Lang Syne" was beautiful; it hit our soft spot. Then, surprisingly, the Brits and Americans in compound #6 all got together and sang the National Anthems of America and England. I had goose bumps all over. There was no way to hold back the tears of emotion. How could we lose, I thought, with all this strength and belief in ourselves and in our purpose? We had to win! Many special private prayers were offered that first night of the New Year.

A few days later, a rumor circulated from the daily signaling that all the Americans and British in solitary, compound #5, would be transferred to a compound like the other prisoners. At last! One of our prayers was being answered, and it couldn't happen too soon. Prisoners were dying too quickly with almost daily funeral parties.

It was my turn to empty the Binjo. As I walked past the other cells on my way to the stairs, I cast a look inside the cells, being careful not to look too long. The guards wanted to get the detail over fast. However, on the way back to my cell, I was able to see a British air crewman who had been burned on the legs, arms, and back, with flies and mosquitoes laying eggs on all the burned spots. The open sores became infected, and within a week and a half, with no medical care, he died. There were many such cases that could have been avoided with just a little care. I cannot forgive such insensitivity and cruelty. Yet I find it equally difficult to condemn a whole nation forever for the actions of its military in wartime. Many nations, including our own, have had similar occasions for which to be ashamed. Malnutrition, torture, and disease were just as final in death as in combat.

For the past few days the boys in the other compounds had been signaling that we were to be moved to another compound and out of our God-forsaken solitary confinement. But when? It could be a week, a month, or more. We waited anxiously; we started to despair. We soon realized that sitting around brooding wasn't going to help us a bit, so we started to tell jokes. Norm Larsen told one that really made me laugh, to the concern of the others. They quickly got me to keep it down, so the guards would not hear us and find a reason to come and beat us. We tossed out that idea and thought up some word games. That proved pretty interesting and a lot quieter. After that, we started to think of jobs that people could start and make a success of themselves. We even thought of a few simple inventions. Things like that helped pass the days, but at times we got tired and irritated at one another over simple things that were quite petty and soon forgotten.

At night we would wear all our clothing, so we wouldn't get bitten by mosquitoes. We were always afraid of catching malaria and other fevers. In the daytime, we wore a G-string, which we fashioned by using a pocket or two from our trousers. The men who were there longer than us had told us to exercise on a regular basis, if possible. We would always see the men who were fit doing their exercises. Those who didn't soon got weak and became ill. I exercised!

What we feared most were a few of the guards. When they got drunk, they came around to frighten us, much to their enjoyment. One afternoon one of the guards who was walking his tour came to our cell and started to jabber about something. We recognized the guard as "Tarzan," who was in charge of our cell block #5. He was the most brutal of all the guards, and at the end of the war, he and twenty two other Japanese officers and prison guards, who had beaten and murdered American soldiers, were rounded up, placed on trial, convicted and hanged. "Tarzan" was the one who dubbed me "American Indian," probably because I had a deep tan and had grown a dense beard. He enjoyed harassing me. This day was not going to be any different.

"Tarzan" poked his rifle at me and said, "Okay doe?" (meaning, "Is it OK ?" When "doe" is added to the end of a phrase, it was always a question.} I didn't know what to say...I half smiled, wondering what would be safe. Should I put on a brave front and say, "OK, shoot me," or should I tell him what I really felt, which was, "No!" Whatever I did say must have upset "Tarzan." He unlocked the cell door.

"'Tomasan'," he ordered me out. I stepped out. He told me to back up a little past the cell. I did.

Then he asked, "OK doe?" Again, I didn't know what to say, and I shrugged. Was the building shaking, or was it just me? My buddies were watching all this from inside their cells, Chet from the cell next to ours. There was nothing they could do or say, not when "Tarzan" was running the show. He lined up the rifle until I looked straight down the barrel just inches from my forehead. A cannon would not have looked any larger. I took a deep breath. He cocked the rifle, sighted again, and slowly pulled the trigger...CLICK...I felt like a burst balloon...Pfftt! He had not loaded the gun and clicked on an empty chamber. Lowering his rifle and grinning from ear to ear with his silver tooth shining, he shoved me back in my cell, locked the door, and went on his way. I hated him;" I wanted to kill him. My buddies managed to calm me down for my own good.

On January 25,1945, we heard the news again that we were going to be moved to another compound. That afternoon, we were taken out of our cells with whatever clothing we had, and told to march in single file to the front yard. Those who were injured, frail, or sick were helped or carried by their buddies. Some prisoners had been imprisoned more than eighteen months. Many in the other compounds had been prisoners much longer. Just looking at those poor souls was heart-rending.

All airmen were taken out of Solitary, #5 compound, and placed in #8 compound, which was a tremendous relief for us all. It afforded Monty the opportunity to expose his arm to the sunshine, and it began healing nicely.

Up to this time, #8 compound was being used to house men from the Indian National Army, who had sided with the Japanese. Since they had to move on to other locations, the compound was available to us. If the fortunes of war had not been changing in favor of the Allies, I doubt that we would have been moved.

One of the Japanese officers gave a short speech, took a head count, and finally led us to our new 'home.' It looked wonderful to us after being cooped up in solitary. At first, we couldn't figure out the reason we had been released from solitary. With all the rumors about the British breakthrough of the Japanese lines in northern Burma, we figured that they thought it would look better for them, if they were overrun, to treat us better. We were in an open area where we could walk around the compound. Once we were inside the new compound, the commandant made a speech, which was translated to us. Basically, it was all the rules and regulations by which we had to abide, or we would all be put back into the cell blocks. His aide assigned two of our boys as 'sooji masters' (cooks), and they, in turn, picked others from the volunteers to be on the cooking detail for the compound. I quickly grabbed that chance for something to do. It proved to be the right decision. Keeping busy was the single most important thing to prevent mind and body from deteriorating.

The diet was the same as in the cell blocks, but we had three pans of rice instead of two every day. We were given rations of rice and "nucca," and some greens about every seven days. We had a small store of wood near the cook shack. The wood wasn't going to last long and we had to be creative about finding some more to cook our rice. Water was also rationed, and if we ran out of anything...too bad! This was certainly a big positive step from the cell blocks. The compounds were shaped like a slice of pie. If put together, they would look like a wagon wheel, which represented the prison; the spaces between the spokes were the compounds. (*Refer to photo of prison on page 48.*)

Each compound had a nine-foot concrete wall along both sides, and an iron-barred fence at both ends. It was good to be out in the sun and to walk around the area. Anyone walking past the narrow end of our compound could see a bit of the rest of the prison through the bars. There was a little building that housed the well and doubled as the medical shack. It wasn't long before we learned another lesson. When we passed this narrow section, there was usually a guard standing or walking by. It was expected that, whenever we were in sight of one, we were to come to attention and bow in the prescribed manner; otherwise we were beaten or made to stand at attention in the hot sun for a few hours without moving or talking.

Every day, at about 0530 A.M., we awoke to the sound of the guard yelling,"Tinkoooo," which meant, roll call. Since we were already clothed in what we'd slept in, it did not take us long to line up in the yard just outside our compound in two rows facing front. The sergeant of the guard would come around with another guard to count and inspect us. Our ranking officer would give the command to count off, and only the front row would do the counting in Japanese. "Ichi, ni, san, shee, go, roko, sitchi, hatchi, koo, joo"...etc. Soon we were quite good at it. Now

The pan was made of galvanized metal and the black Bakelite bowl was for
liquids. We scratched squares with numbers in each square on the back of the
pan for Bingo. Of course we always had the same numbers. With my
homemade knife, I carved a fork, spoon and a pipe. In solitary, I picked up a
broken piece of bamboo when I went out to dump the Binjo.

the last man had two words that he could say. If the two lines ended
evenly, he would call out, '*Itzi gitzu.*' However, if the lines ended
unevenly, he would say, '*Mong.*' I remember one of those mornings we
counted off and the last man, Hank Pisterzi, was the odd man, so out
came this loud 'MONNNNNG'. His voice made the '*ONG*' vibrate
longer that it should have. Paradoxically, in the midst of misery, there
is humor. I had to force myself not to burst out laughing. The guards,
who wanted firm, snappy calls, made it clear that Hank's version would
not be tolerated. He was lucky he wasn't beaten. At 1900 P.M. each
day, we would repeat the procedure.

The men who didn't work on the cooking detail did other things to keep themselves busy. They'd sweep out the cells with home-made brooms, and dust the bars and other areas with parts of their clothing. It felt better to have things a little cleaner. Soon, the boys started a checker tournament. The checkers were made from the spines of fish. Once in a while we would get some dried salted fish crawling with worms...the closest we got to surf-and-turf. I'd always liked checkers, so I entered the competition. I lasted two rounds until Ozzie, a New Zealander, beat me. There was only one hand-made chess set in our compound, until Grady Farley and I decided to make our own set. We carved and scraped dark pieces out of teakwood and pieces out of light sandstone. In Burma teakwood was as common as our pine. Sandstone we picked up around the yard. For a chessboard, we used the concrete floors and scratched in the boxes. One of the men got a piece of galvanized metal from the outhouse area and, by bending the piece back and forth enough times, ended up with a square shape for the board. I remember scratching squares and numbers on the bottom of my rice pan to play Bingo. Of course, we always played with the same numbers.

Chet and some others taught the fundamentals of chess to whoever was interested. Finally, enough of us had learned the basics to start a tournament. It not only lightened the atmosphere and made the time go swiftly but also helped to heal our brain cells for a short time. I won my first match but lost the next one to my co-pilot, Chet Paul. A month later, he won the contest. Prize? Winning was enough.

It was encouraging to see improvement in some of the boys, who had been in solitary cell-blocks for up to eighteen months. That was a long time, and it had left its mark on their bodies and minds. The warm sun was the light of freedom bathing them and helping them to try to forget those dingy, dark, cell-blocks in solitary. For others, it was just a prolonged agony, after which they died. At first, I couldn't understand why a grown man could not pull himself together and somehow endure the prison life if he weren't sick or injured. I soon learned that being sick or injured was a condition I could see, and so I'd understood why the men were having trouble coping. What I hadn't comprehended was the mental and emotional injuries of a man who appeared not to have any problems. It was agonizing to see such a man deteriorate before my eyes as he withdrew further and further into a hopeless shell, giving up on life and dying before his time.

I wanted to help many, but there was little I could do to reach through anyone's depression and pull him out of his misery. Compassion for those who could not help themselves was the painful lesson I learned from these men. I vowed always to think positively and not to tolerate negative thoughts in my mind or in the minds of my buddies. Negative thoughts were self-defeating and, in our unbearable situation, life-threatening. This makes one a very intolerant man. My wife can attest to what she's had to endure due to my intolerance That vow, out of necessity, has been somewhat modified in my life today.

After a short time in our new compound, we became aware of a small brick building in a corner about the width of a small, one-car garage and twice as long. There were two entrances to this little nine by thirty- foot room. The main entrance was outside our compound, but a smaller one lay within our walls. The Japanese used only the main entrance. The back door was always padlocked. Upon curious inspection, we discovered that this was the Japanese storehouse for their food. We could have found a way to break the lock, but that would have complicated matters if a guard had spotted it. One of our men managed to chip away at the padlock assembly, which was imbedded in the brickwork. With great cunning and ingenuity, and because the building was visible, it took about two weeks to complete. Finally it was done; the way it worked was just great. All we had to do was to remove one brick, and the whole hinge section came out and hung freely.

We all decided that only in emergencies, after assessment of the severity of an illness by our commander, a few of us at great risk would sneak quietly into the room for food. It was a life-and-death decision. We knew there was food in there, and it was obvious that we couldn't take large amounts of food without being noticed. The penalty for that would have been quite severe and would have jeopardized any plans we had to help our sick comrades. Someone would open the door and quickly take what was needed--usually an egg or two--and just as quietly go back, shut the door, replace the hinge section, and put the brick in place. For some, it sustained life; for others it was too late. A few who died would have been alive today if they had been able to hang on for three or four weeks longer. Their cards of life had been played out.

Three or four weeks, such a short time! For these dying men, though, it was an eternity. It was a slow, grinding cycle, because there were definite steps in the weakening and decaying of the body and mind. Wounds from our last battle: dysentery, malaria, beri-beri, dengue fever, the ever present itch, that when aggravated, usually started an epidemic of sores, developing into skin ulcers—all were a part of the agonizing cycle. Last but not least were the Japanese themselves with their beatings and the meager diet, rationed out to us. There's nothing invented by man that can overshadow the abuse which our bodies sustained.

As time stretched, for some into years, and for our B-29 men it stretched into many months, our hopes started to dim. Everyone realized that we had to find new thoughts to occupy our minds. We continued our light exercises to help tone up our bodies as best we could. Our first weeks in the new compound were spent searching casually, so as not to attract any attention, in all corners of the yard for anything that could be of any use to us. Pieces of metal were fashioned into spoons, forks, and knives. I managed to find a piece of an old, rusted barrel hoop from which I ground a rough blade. I kept walking back and forth along the cement wall of our compound, shaping the thin piece of metal. I had to be careful that the guards didn't notice what I was doing. Usually three or four men would casually walk with me and I would hold the blade against the wall while I walked and talked with the fellows. It was shaping up pretty well after a week. I hardened the metal by placing it in the fire of the cook shack when we were cooking, then quickly putting it into the water trough. Now I needed a handle. I got a short piece of bamboo from our pile of firewood and using the crude knife, cut a 3" length, split it down the middle lengthwise, and placed the blade between the pieces. With an old shoelace, I bound and tied the pieces together as tightly as I could. Then I wet the whole handle and let it dry in the sun. It held together just fine.

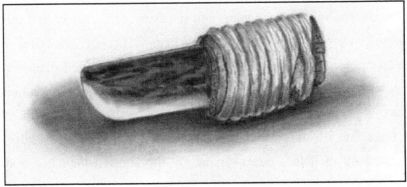

The knife I made that helped me be useful.

We had heard that this compound had been occupied by the Indian National Army. Since they weren't prisoners, they'd used it as their barracks. When my radio operator, Richard Brooks, was idly searching the areas on top of the cross beams on the outside of our compound, he ran across a honing stone. What a miracle! It was just what I needed to give my rough blade a fine sharp edge. I tempered it in the cooking fire and honed it until the blade was razor sharp. When I gave someone a shave, it proved a great success! Soon I had a regular stream of customers. It was great, and it was something that made me feel useful. I think the one I worried about most was the haircut that I gave to 'Ozzie,' my New Zealander friend. He wanted a completely shaven head, and I was very worried that I might accidently cut him on the soft skin of the scalp. I took the time to boil the water and had it at the ready. When I did cut him twice, I quickly cleansed the cuts with the boiled water. They never got infected. I went on to give about eighty shaves and sixty haircuts and trims. A slight scratch could get infected and end up as a full-fledged skin ulcer. Case in point: at night, we would put on clothes to present fewer open area for mosquitos. One night as I was sleeping, my ankle became itchy. I must have scratched it with the heel of my GI shoes. Even though I had worn my socks, I irritated the bite enough to break the skin. The next day it was infected. I tried keeping it in check by cleaning it with boiling water day and night and swatting the flies away. The mosquitoes and flies seemed to make a straight line for my infections. I would tie a little piece of fabric just over the sore to keep them off as I walked, but it was a losing battle. Slowly but surely, the sores got larger, deeper, and very painful. Giving shaves and haircuts meant standing on my feet, which built up pressure and pain on my ankle. I had to rest after each shave, and realized I was being limited and debilitated with the sores. I rested when I could.

When I started to feel chills, I knew I was experiencing my first malaria attack. The guys piled up whatever clothes we had to cover me, but that did not seem to lessen the chills. I felt as if I had a high temperature and would start sweating profusely. I lost a lot of weight, which worried me, but with the supportive care of my buddies, I found the courage and determination to get well. These attacks happened intermittently for the rest of my captivity. Days later after my recuperation, I started carving and building things out of bamboo strips. Richard Brooks and I made a crude table for eating meals. It looked odd! There it was, and we could not sit by it... no seats. We got some loose bricks and limbs of bamboo, tied the pieces together with vines, and made two chairs. Two men had 4" saws, which they had kept from their escape kit before they were captured and smuggled through all the time they'd been prisoners. We finally had everything ready for our first meal at our table.

As we sat down with our metal pans, my thoughts once more wandered home. I could see my folks around the dining table with Grandma saying a prayer. If only I were home and could tell them that I was alive and O.K. What my stomach wouldn't have given for a nice juicy steak with fried onions and Armenian pilaf. Pilaf is rice, but in no way, was it the rice we had in prison with our meat delicacy, rice bugs. Since we came into this compound, we'd gotten three-quarters of a leg of pork every thirty to forty-five days. Divide that among over a hundred people. Nobody ends up with much nutrition. We cut the pork into tiny cubes, put them in the soup or mixed them in with the rice. Pretty soon, arguments came up that someone had gotten one or two pieces more than the other fellow. We rarely got meat, which made it harder for some men to accept the portion dealt to them. I personally couldn't see any point in arguing. If one didn't get much this time, he would probably make it up next time. I realized that everybody wasn't thinking rationally, so how could I expect logical thinking? Some of the prisoners' minds were weakened to that of a child. It was sad. Had I been a prisoner for two or three years, as some of these men had been, who knows in what condition I would have been? I tried my best to understand their reactions, help them in their despair, comfort them in their agonies. This all had an impact on the person I am today.

About this time, we started to run short of firewood for the cook shack. The Japs weren't giving us the full ration of wood needed to cook the rice and boil the water for drinking. One of the British officers, who had been an engineer, used the trap door in the ceiling that led to the rafters of our compound. He climbed up the inner wooden bars, which reached from floor to ceiling. We gave him a boost to start up the bars and watched the front gate in case the Japs surprised us again. Once he was through the trap door, he studied the structure and came up with a plan. He marked the support beams which could be removed without the roof collapsing. Now we needed a foot-long saw. Captain Myers was the man to make it. He got a piece of corrugated metal from the partitions in the latrine area and was able to fashion a crude saw for us. Brooks volunteered to climb up through the trap door and started cutting the marked beams. All was going well when, suddenly, the Japs entered our compound and ordered a surprise roll call. Brooks was told to stop sawing and to keep very quiet. Everyone lined up in two rows, and by keeping it a bit loose near the end of the line, we ended up with the same count as we had in the morning roll call. Thank you, God! We'd gotten away with it. The Jap guards left, and Brooks continued sawing. After the beam was finally sawed through, he sawed it into smaller pieces. From that time on, we repeated this procedure until the end of our captivity. We wondered why the guards did not question where we got our firewood. Once we knew we had a source for the wood, we never brought up the subject of firewood to the guards, and somehow it just slid by unnoticed.

Due to the acute meat shortage, someone noticed one day all the sparrows flying around our compound, and got the bright idea to trap them for food. A prisoner made a trap by using a piece of wire mesh, which he tore off an old, broken-down cage, and stretched it over strips of bamboo. He ended up with a two-by-three-foot screen, which was held down at one end by a rock and on the other propped up by a thin piece of bamboo, the bottom of which had a string tied to it. Then he sprinkled some rice, just a little bit, in the center of the target area. After a long wait, a bird saw the rice and came to nibble. The string was pulled and, WHOOM, the trap fell on the bird. There was a mad scramble for the trap. Whoever had pulled the string got the bird and finished the job. He cleaned it, barbecued it, and said it tasted wonderful. After a few days of this, Brooks and I thought we might as well try it ourselves.

We borrowed one of the traps, set it up, and waited...and waited. Finally a few birds came down and pecked around. We held our breaths, not making a sound. Suddenly, one sparrow hopped in and started pecking at the rice. I quickly jerked the string and captured it. Carefully, I reached under the screen, grabbed the bird, and pulled it out. My! It was so small and cute as it chirped and chirped and blinked its eyes. Now, I had to take hold of the head, grab the rest of the body at the neck with the other hand, and with a quick twist, wrench off the head. It was so nice and warm in my hands. There couldn't have been but a few, very small pieces of meat on the whole bird. A sudden urge came over me to free it. The sparrow's predicament was the same as mine. The few men watching me noted that I was hesitating. One of them, Captain Hunt, said, "If you don't want the bird, I'll take it."

I gave the sparrow over to him. It wasn't long before he was cooking it over the fire for his next meal.

That was not the end of our search for food. A few days later, while Brooks was looking at some pigeons flying around, he noted that they perched under the eaves of the roof of our compound. He thought of a plan to catch them. We climbed up to the ceiling of the second floor, crawled through an opening we had made there earlier when we were looking for wood to burn in our cook shack. Then we crawled along the supports of the roof with makeshift clubs which e had brought along. It was dark, dirty, and full of cobwebs. There we were, clothed in nothing more than our improvised loin cloths. Finally, Brooks and I came upon one of the nests which was along the edge of the ceiling where the roof sloped down to meet the outer wall. The pigeons would fly under the eaves and into their nests. Brooks went a little farther and found another nest. We both waited silently with our clubs raised. We straddled the beams for more than an hour, waiting. My conscience is clear today. No pigeons came. Climbing back down, we looked at each other and laughed. Boy...were we dirty and sweaty from the heat and filth under that hot roof. If only it had rained, we could all stand under the down spouts and have a good shower. It would have felt great even without soap. Needless to say, we did not broadcast this little episode to anyone.

It was remarkable what we fashioned out of galvanized sheet metal. Even the tools we used had to be made first. Simple accomplishments were profound. Our creativity was stretched to unknown limits, and our handiwork, started from almost nothing, developed our construction capabilities. I remember when Captain Meyer made a padlock out of the sheet metal he pried off of the latrine wall. It was about three inches by five and half inches thick. It even had a key that worked. I was impressed. We all made different types of things just to keep busy. I was still giving shaves and haircuts with the blade that I had made. Thank God for that honing stone.

By now, it was only the middle of March 1945. Time was passing slowly. Every day, I would tend to my skin ulcers as best I could with boiling water. It was a tedious and painful ritual, which I had to repeat by dipping a small piece of cloth from my clothing into the hot water and swabbing the pus from the sores until they were clear. When I had dysentery, I'd run for the Binjo. Our only remedy for dysentery was to swallow charcoal and wash it down with pre-boiled water. The bottoms of my feet were toughened, but my ankles were swollen from the ulcers and caused me pain when I stood for long periods or walked. In spite of the pain, I walked and did some light exercise to keep my body ready for any eventuality. I didn't know what I would be called upon to do.

At random, a guard would open the gate, walk in, pick one or more of the men, and start beating them. At other times, the guard would have a man tied to the iron fencing at the head of the compound and leave him there all day without food or water. We were not allowed to give him water or talk to him, or we would wind up next to him. With the hot sun beating down on the prisoner all day, he would become acutely dehydrated and sunburned by the time the guards finally untied him from the fence. These atrocities went on throughout March and April. Rumors of the British advancing south from Mandalay began to hit our network of prison communication. Patiently, with rising anticipation, we waited. Those rumors kept us alive. There were moments of great hope mingled with days of despair. Strong courage, endurance, and a determined will to live were necessary for survival. Ingenuity, sacrifice, and tolerance had to be developed by every prisoner. God became known to every man.

On my routine walk one morning within the prison compound, I noticed it–a thin, delicate shoot of greenery, pushing its way up through the stones and the rubble of the barren ground. I stooped down, gently clearing away debris from the tendril, aerating the soil around it. Here was a sign of hope...a new, fresh, living symbol of life. Could it be kept alive for us to enjoy the beauty of the bloom? I told a few of my fellow prisoners. They came over to watch in growing curiosity. As the routine of care continued day after day, a bud soon appeared, and bets were made as to which color and type of flower into which it would bloom.

Easter morning dawned on Sunday April 1, 1945. After roll call, the guards left the compound without incident. We went to see our flower...it had blossomed...a white lily, pristine and so beautiful.

Imagine, of all the flowers in the blooming kingdom, why a lily...and a white one at that! Unbelievable emotion overcame me.   I cut the flower and stem at ground level with my shaving blade and took it to our chaplain, Lt. Lionel Coffin. He was arranging a makeshift altar for our Easter service on the second floor of our compound. He took the lily, carefully placed it in a bamboo cup, and set it on the altar: no explanations, just a symbol of hope amid all the suffering.

Nearly 100 men had to gather on the second floor without attracting the attention of the guards. How were we to accomplish this? The Japs had made it quite clear that we were not to gather even in small groups...and 100 men is not a small group. Before we had time to think of a solution, the Jewish prisoners, all twelve of them, quickly offered a solution. They would make themselves very visible by walking around and climbing up and down the outer stairs while we had our Easter service. The risk of being caught was ever present, and only God knew what the punishment would be. At the very least it would have been beatings for everyone. I will never forget their unselfish bravery.

Slowly, we gathered, and as we settled down and waited for the sermon to begin, all eyes went to the altar. There, in the middle of the crude table, was the lily. Tears were shed unabashedly. Thoughts of home engulfed us. Was this a trick of fate? ...Or was it truly a symbol of hope? Oh, did we pray! As surely as that lily bloomed, we knew we would regain our freedom. Five weeks later...WE DID!

After our service had ended, those of the Jewish faith changed places with us for their service. Covering for them was easy for us and not nearly as dangerous, with so many people to mill around.

On April 8, I celebrated my twenty-first birthday. A small cake made of cooked rice squeezed into the shape of a tennis ball was cut in half. Everyone quietly sang "Happy Birthday". Again, thoughts of home filled my mind. How I wished I could let my parents and grandmother know that I was alive. It worried me that they might not know anything. As the days and weeks dragged on, strong rumors flew around and around the prison that a major landing would be made by the British, but we had no concrete information. Suddenly, our guards became busy with a lot of hurried activity in their area.

For nine months my mother could not bring herself to write in her diary, then word reached her that I was missing in action, 'MIA'. She continued her diary:

April 23ʳᵈ 1945

   My darling, where are you? Since you went overseas, I became more and more restless and less courageous. I didn't want to continue this "Diary", because I was afraid to write thoughts quite unpleasant and depressing. I admit, for many times I was tempted to start this daily recording of a few lines, but somehow I stayed short of courage.

   YOU ARE MISSING SINCE DECEMBER 14ᵗʰ. Oh! My Darling, your poor Mom and Pop are certainly very brave, but most of the time during the day, I feel sort of a lump in my throat. You are missing! I shall never forget the shock that I went through.

   You are missing, for us, yes! But here is where we must arm ourselves with faith and courage and patience, and what not! For us you are missing, but God is with you, that's certain. HE WILL BRING YOU TO US AGAIN.

Pop and I shall suffer untold feelings of anxiety and uncertainty, but never mind our sufferings. I am willing to suffer and suffer, and hope that some day, (Oh God make it soon.) I will hear from you again. You are missing! God is your supreme guardian.

April 24th

Do you want me to describe here some of my mental tortures? The very first days I became just like a dumb, good for nothing person. No appetite, no sleep, lost weight and I became all of a sudden a silent person! I admit that your Grandma was very brave and she is still brave and courageous. Your Pop is also courageous. In fact, the three of us avoid to sentimentalize about you. We spare each other, and that helps us to make the home atmosphere bearable. I admit that I cry many times during the day, but nobody sees me in that condition. The bathroom and my bedroom and Washington Heights' quiet corners in the park will tell you some day about all the tears I shed, and how I prayed to God for your life and safety.

April 25th

I shall never forget the kindness and the goodness of all our friends. Karnik my darling, at least we can say we are fortunate people to possess such wonderful and sincere friends. The Jeffersons specially were simply more than friends. I hope some day we can repay their kindness in someway very pleasant to them. Their swell little girl, Daisy, is really your true friend. It makes us feel so good to feel that we have such good and sincere friends.

It will take me many pages to write down all the names of all our friends who were and are so nice to us. They all feel about you as if you were their own son. So you can imagine what Pop and I feel about you, for you are our son, our only and precious darling, so good, so kind, so young, you are the very essence of our lives. Oh Karnik, hurry up! Tell us where you are.
...you see, I seem not yet ready and reasonable to write. I am becoming such an unreasonable mother. I know you are more than anxious to get in touch with your parents. Good night for this evening.

April 26, 1945: The guards came into our compound and had us line up for roll call. We called out our numbers and waited with great anticipation. What was happening? The commandant told us through an interpreter, that they (The Japanese) were marching away from Rangoon. They were going to take all able-bodied men who could march to leave with them. A special formation and a formal inspection by a Japanese doctor and several officers made us uneasy. We were uneasy without knowing why, since attention of this sort by the doctor had never before happened. The rest of the day was uneventful. We had our roll call, ate our rice, and prayed we all had made the right decisions about the march. We would decide tonight who of us were fit and strong enough to march and who were not. After a few words with our leaders, the Japs left. Those who were able to walk had no decision to make...they had to go. Those who were on their backs had to remain behind. Some of us were borderline...we could walk, but for how long and under what conditions? Should we stay...with the possibility that we might be killed...or would the Japs just leave us to fend for ourselves, totally defenseless? If we went on the march, could we last? My ankle sores were not healing well, and I feared that if I went on the march, I might not be able to keep up with the rest. If so, would I be shot on the side of the road? I agonized over the possibilities and decided to stay and help the really sick ones. Everyone slept fitfully, full of anxious doubts and private indecisions about tomorrow.

April 27th

    Karnig my boy, I feel so sure that you are safe and well under God's incomprehensible protection. Do you know that every single day, twice a day, I hope to get some news from you? Well sooner or later I will hear from you! God bless my darling. Smile please! God is with us. Here is hope and courage for you, your parents and your Grandma!

April 28, 1945: We got up at the usual time, but on this day, our guards dumped a large supply of clothes and shoes into the compound.

We were told to find clothes that would fit us. The jackets were Japanese Army issue and so were the pants, which resembled culottes. The shoes were sneakers, rubber and canvas, with the big toe separated from the other toes. The guards wanted the ones who were going on the march to wear the regular Japanese army clothes. When they left our compound, a few of our comedians relieved some of the tension of the moment. I particularly remember Sgt. Hill, a cockney lad from England, who chose one of the uniforms that fit him and started to prance around like the Japs. He had a false tooth right in the center of the upper row of his mouth, and he was able to push it out with his tongue so that it rested on his lower lip. Thank God the guards didn't see him, or they would have shot him right there.

By noon everyone was ready. The Japs gathered the prisoners from each compound and assembled all 430 of them in the courtyard. There were a few carts laden with the Japanese supplies, which the prisoners would have to push and pull. I still had my G.I. shoes, but with my swollen feet and ankles they wouldn't fit, so I gave my shoes to Brooks, and we repeated our wishes, said our good-byes, gave our hugs, and prayed we would all see each other again. Suddenly, they were gone! There was a stillness in the air. Anxiously, we waited and wondered what was going to happen next.

The following excerpts are from Norman Larson's and Nicholas Oglesby's recollections of the march from Rangoon.

Norman recalls: "We left Rangoon Central Prison and marched through the streets of Rangoon. At the head of the column strode British Brigadier Clive Hopson, walking stick under his arm, marching erect as a West Point cadet. At his side, equally erect, strode the Japanese commandant known to Japanese soldiers and us alike as the 'Big Tai.' At the tail end of the column was the motley gang of Air Corps people, most of whom walked barefooted.

"We were forced to pull a couple of large two-wheeled bullock carts loaded down with Japanese supplies. As I recall, a group of about ten of us took turns pulling each cart. We marched for about fifty minutes and rested ten minutes. Every time we stopped, all of us would drop to the ground. We continued the march all through that night and were exhausted long before dawn. Everybody more or less got through the first night's march, and in the morning we made camp in what appeared to be some sort of military bivouac area. We were fed a rather generous portion of rice and tea, and thought that things weren't all that bad. Little did I know that was all we would have until the night of the 29th."

Norman recalled: "For the next three nights and days all they had to eat was what they could liberate from the bullock carts. This was a precarious and dangerous undertaking because, if caught, the penalty would have been rather severe...and permanent.

"Chet Paul and his buddy Joe Levine (bombardier on Meyer's crew) swiped a couple of raw onions. Somebody else got a very sweet substance which looked almost like fudge. In his one attempt at pilferage, all he got for his effort was one Burmese cheroot (like a cigar)."

Nick Oglesby recalls; "We marched up the road towards Mandalay in the moonlight, many of us barefooted. My Japanese shoes were unwearable, because my feet had swelled from being barefooted all the time. The shoes caused blisters on my heels, so I discarded them. It wasn't too bad on a paved road, but marching at night with only the light from the moon lighting our way was difficult. Our biggest fear was that we would be spotted by allied aircraft, and we were sure that our own people would have no idea that we were prisoners of war."

Norman writes: "In this connection, I remember a bit of black humor. When we heard the roar of an approaching aircraft, the cry invariably would go up, 'Is it friendly or one of ours?'

"Early on there had been a few successful escapes by the people in the groups ahead of us. Many of us had formed small four or five man escape units and were planning to take off at the opportune moment. However the Big Tai put a quick stop to this. He passed the word back that if anyone escaped, ten people were to be picked at random from the group with whom he was marching and shot. Brigadier Hopson, in order to protect our own people from being shot, passed the order that anyone who escaped would be subject to court martial. That was the end of the escapes for the time being."

Norman goes on to say: "As extreme hunger, thirst, and fatigue took over, our conditions became desperate. One of our guys, Lou Bishop, a P-40 pilot and long-term POW, developed a severe case of diarrhea. He was dropping further and further behind the column and was using those precious and infrequent rest periods to catch up with the rest of us. When I wasn't pulling one of the bullock carts, I dropped back to help Lou. I soon found that it was more than I could do to stay with him all night. I got four or five of the other guys to take turns helping him. Incredibly, he somehow managed to get through the march.

"As the nights dragged on, some of the men from the groups ahead of us were dropping out. We passed these pathetic looking creatures who were sitting at the side of the road. The word was that they would be picked up by trucks and brought back to the POW prison in Rangoon. In actuality they were picked up by Japanese soldiers and immediately shot and killed.

"One of the things I worried about was falling asleep during a rest period and not waking up promptly when the order came to resume marching. I am a world class sleeper and can sleep through practically anything. Back at Rangoon one hot night with no breeze, some of the guys were sleeping outside the building and were caught by the guards. The guards came into our compound, beat up these guys, and then came through the rooms upstairs where I was sleeping. They came in and lashed out at random hitting half a dozen of our guys. There was a great deal of noise and shouting going on, but I blissfully slept through the whole thing.

"In the morning, after the third night's march, our group was hiding out in a small grove of trees a couple of hundred yard from the road. The sounds of aircraft were now almost constant. Flight after flight of P-51s went zooming by a hundred or so feet over our heads. It seemed like almost a miracle that they didn't spot us.

"Later that morning we got the word that the Japs were abandoning the bullock carts. The events of the last night of marching are somewhat blurred. The complete lack of sleep and of rice and tea was pushing all of us to the very edge of complete exhaustion. How some of the weaker prisoners ever made it through that night is almost incomprehensible. Not having to pull those cursed bullock carts any longer helped a bit.

"During the early morning hours we walked through the bombed out city of Pegu. It was only a shell and I didn't see one living creature. It was kind of eerie. At one point the column had to go around a hole in the middle of the road. In the hole was crouched a Jap soldier cradling a rather large bomb. The Brits later told us that this was a KamiKaze booby trap. When a British tank or truck went over the hole, the Jap would detonate the bomb and detonate himself and the British equipment to bits."

Nickolas recalls: "Shortly after daybreak, we were given the news that the Japanese guards had left us. They had given a written document to the ranking officer, British Brigadier General Hopson, passing the command of the prisoner detachment to him.

"We were free, but we were behind the Japanese lines with Japanese troops all around us. They were attempting to get to the safety of the mainland of Asia before the British Eighth Army overran their units.

"While we were certain the British knew exactly where we were, we felt we needed to pinpoint our present location so they could plan our rescue operation more easily. We arranged large, white cloth panels, as best we could with what we had on the ground outside the village wooded area, hoping that they would realize that POW personnel were here."

Norman writes: "It took a few minutes to come down to earth and to realize that our situation wasn't all that great. There was a Japanese Army between us and the British 14th Army. If the Japanese retreated back through our village, they could easily wipe us all out. On the other hand the British, in the mistaken belief that we were the enemy, could also shell and shoot the hell out of us.

"We lit a stack of hay, waved pieces of white cloth to attract the British fighters, but to no avail. A group of British Hurricanes were flying at about 2-3,000 feet and saw all this commotion on the ground. They contacted their base and told them about it. Some guy at the base said it's a lot of baloney, it's a Japanese trick; all the POWs are back in Rangoon. Go in and hit them. That is precisely what the Hurricanes did.

"Before the raid started, I had heard that a first aid station had been set up underneath the Burmese basha, which the Brigadier had taken over as his headquarters. I had gone there to take care of my heel, which by now was aching continuously. They could do nothing for it. That is when I heard the sound of machine gun fire from the Hurricanes. I dived behind a huge tree which was next to the basha. The bullets slammed into the tree and also hit the Brigadier, killing him instantly.

"After the first wave passed, I made a dash across an open field for a bomb crater that I remembered seeing when we came to the village that morning. I was almost there when the fighters made another pass. With no place to hide, I just lay flat on the ground and waited for the worst to happen. A line of bullets plowed up the dirt no more than a foot from my head. After that pass I did manage to get into the bomb crater, which by now was full of guys, and in fact several came in on top of me which was quite comforting. Incredibly, the only person killed in the raid was Brigadier Clive Hopson. The brigadier had been captured in Singapore early in 1942. He had endured over three years of Japanese imprisonment, and now he had been killed by his own people a few hours after liberation. How ironic!"

Back at Rangoon Central Prison, we were all wondering what was going to happen next. Soon I saw a guard making his rounds, but he looked strange. The third time he passed in front, I cautiously went to the front iron fence and bowed properly. He stopped and acknowledged me.

I proceeded to ask him, "Are prisoners other compounds?" in broken English.

To my surprise, he answered me in perfect English, "Yes, there are more in other compounds."

He was very young, wore clean clothes and thick glasses. He was not like the others, and I felt that he didn't want to be there any more than I did...probably did clerical work. That day went quietly but with an underlying tension.

April 29, 1945: This day was uneventful as well. As night fell, Cliff Emeny, an R.A.F. fighter pilot from New Zealand, and I were sitting high on the compound steps, looking out over the walls to the city beyond. I was smoking a tea leaf cigarette I had rolled, while Cliff and I talked about our present situation. It was a clear, moonlit night, and we could see fires and small explosions all over the city of Rangoon. Obviously, the Japs were destroying all they could before the Allies got there.

Suddenly, I realized that I had not seen a guard in over an hour.

"Cliff, have you seen a guard lately?" I asked.

"No, I haven't,"answered Cliff. "That's unusual. Let's go down and take a look around to make sure...they may have gone."

We waited a bit more, then moved cautiously down the steps and over to the Jap storeroom in one corner of our compound. If we went into the small building, we would be able to get a clear view of the front gate through the front window of the building. Carefully we removed the loosened brick, swung the lock assembly out from the wall, opened the door, and went to the front window. We kept very quiet. We could see clearly through the entranceway of the prison and right out to the city street. The large teakwood doors were wide open. The only light was from two bare small bulbs—one on each side wall. After standing there about twenty minutes, making sure there was nobody about, we hurried back and told Wing Commander Hudson about our discovery. He was now the ranking officer in our compound. We kept it all pretty quiet so that the men would not get overly excited until we made sure that all the Japs had left.

A decision was made to scale the seven foot inner wall, to assess the situation. Seven of us, including W/C Hudson, hiked each other over the wall. In my zeal to get over fast, I forgot to reach back and grab Gus Johnson's hand to pull him up.

He quietly called to me, "Hey, Tommy, give me a hand!"

I was able to reach back, with the aid of others, to help him up. (After all these years, Gus has never let me forget that oversight. We still laugh over it.) When I pulled Gus up, my shoulders still ached from my parachute jump, but who cared? Now, we were on the outside of our compound, and in the area where guards and trucks had traveled throughout the prison. A few of us went towards the main gate to check it out, while the others went to the front iron gates of our compound and found a note which the fleeing guards had left on the gate. They opened the envelope and read the message.

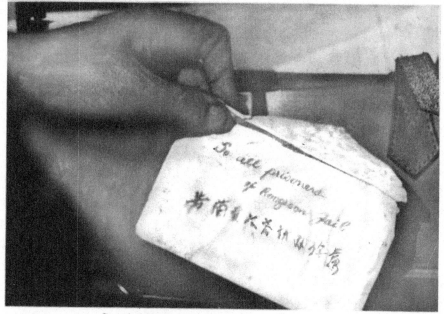

Guards left this envelope on the compound gate
with letter to all prisoners before they fled.

APRIL 29, 1945
JAPS GONE....WE'RE FREE!

The following are the exact typewritten words.

To:

Gentlmen, Bravely you have come here opening prison. We have
gone. keeping you prisnors safely with Nipponese Knightship.
Aferwards we may meet again at the frunt somewhere. then let us
fight bravely each other.
Nippinese Army
(We have kept the gate keys at the gate room)

We were wary of going directly to the main front gate of the prison, fearing that the area might be mined. Some of the British got together, and from the fields beyond the compounds, coaxed a cow to walk through the entrance of the prison. The cow took her time meandering aimlessly through the large arched entranceway and right out onto the dark city street outside. No explosions, no mines. We quickly ran to the large front doors, pulled them shut, and locked them. Some of the others and I went scurrying around the Jap quarters, looking for guns and ammunition to protect ourselves from the Burmese. The city of Rangoon was in desperate need of food. Had the natives known that the Japs had left, the people would have poured into the prison and taken what little the Japs had left for us. It was fortunate for us that this all happened after midnight, while the city slept. The next morning was quite different. Almost a thousand people milled around outside the prison walls. We all prayed for the British to come soon.

I found a rifle, some rounds of ammunition, and two hand grenades, which I gave to one of the other men. I also found an ivory cigarette holder that had a decorative design carved into it. Though I don't smoke, I kept it, and still have it today. After we found a few more rifles and ammo and more grenades, we took turns guarding the two barred windows up front on either side of the main gate. We were so excited, we couldn't sleep. Our minds raced with all the possible scenarios that could happen. Day dawned. We must have been living on adrenalin. During all this excitement, I neglected my duties in helping to prepare the morning rice and nucca, but it got prepared by someone else. My duty now was to be part of a small group of men who were able to find arms to guard the front gate. We also stationed two men on the upper floors above the entrance. We could now cover a much larger area so that nobody could surprise us.

During the evening another letter was found in the guard room. Following are the exact words as they were typed:

Rangoon 29, April 1945

To the whole captured prisnors of Rangoon Jail.

According to the Nippinese order, We hereby give you liberty and admit to leave this place at your own will.

Regarding food and other materials kept in this compound we give you permission to consume them as far as your necessity is concerned.

We hope that we shall have an opportunity to meet you again at battlefield of somewhere.

We shall continue our war efforts eternally in order to get the emancipation of all Asiatic Races.

> *Harvo ITO*
> *The chief Officer of*
> *Rangoon Branch*

We laughed at both letters and also had a feeling of relief, that now we were on our own, without any guards who could harm us. We kept the letters for posterity and continued our watch. Though the Japs had gone, we were still not out of danger. The Burmese were always at the front main gate of the prison. Soon we had a conversation with a responsible Burmese businessman. He kept us informed about the advances of the British armies forging south towards Rangoon.

April 29th from Mom's diary.

I felt so miserable on Easter Day, April 1st. For the first time since you went, I was not able to control my over tired nerves and feelings. I went to church in the morning. Each time I go to church, I break down. On this special Easter Sunday, believe me I could cry aloud even in the church. I came home and went to my room and had a long good cry. Daisy caught me in that condition. The nice little darling, she felt very bad and miserable. All she could do was to hold me tight and say nothing. She brought me a nice little present too. Pop came from church too. I couldn't take any lunch almost all day long. I felt very miserable, what an Easter! Are we going to have a real Easter of resurrection of our own?

April 30, 1945: The British 14th Army was still fighting the Japanese Army near Pegu, about 50 miles north of Rangoon. Major General Matsui had just received a communique from his superior, Lieutenant General Kimura, ordering him to return to Rangoon with his brigade "with all speed and defend it to the death." Kimura, after abandoning Rangoon, was now relatively safe in Moulmein. Matsui had no intention of becoming an immortal hero. Instead, he led his brigade of 'amateurs' away from certain annihilation and took off at night into the hills of the Pegu Yomas to regroup.

April 30th
The other day in town I met your Co-Pilots' mother, Mrs. Paul. We talked of nothing else but of our boys. We promised each other to keep our hopes and chins high. We sent some little sun suits to the babies of Mrs. Parmalee and Mrs. McCutcheon.

May 1, 1945: Commanding Officer Lionel Hudson sent Cliff Emeny, Ed Dow and me to accompany the Burmese civilian, who had been helping us across the river to the native sections on the other side. He would be our guide and interpreter. We tried to enlist the natives' help, gathering all available sturdy boats, should the advancing British armies need boats to cross the river to reach our prison. The Burmese man and Cliff did all the negotiating, while Ed and I kept our Jap rifles ready in case we ran into any unexpected trouble. The natives invited us into their huts and put some food and drink in front of us, but we declined the offer. We were warned not to eat or drink anything, because our stomachs would not be able to handle it. We had to be careful that our water was boiled, and that any food, fruits, and vegetables were properly cleaned.

After we finished making the proper arrangements, we hopped into the canoe, rowed back across the river, and walked back to the Rangoon Central Jail. After Cliff reported to the CO, we went our separate ways, visiting the other compounds and getting our skin ulcers tended to by the British doctor. He had a blue stone which he wet and put on the ulcer. It smarted and stung but helped a bit. I was still hobbling from the pain. My ankles were still swollen, probably from the beri-beri.

During the day a few Brits somehow got onto the roof of compound #1, and with a kind of white-wash made with ground up rice mixed with water, painted the words JAPS GONE. The British fighter pilots apparently didn't believe it, because an RAF Mosquito bomber let a bomb go, that hit the outer wall but fortunately did not injure anyone. The Brits, again, quickly climbed onto the roof of compound # 7, and painted the words EXTRACT DIGIT. It worked! The British pilots got the message and wig-wagged their wings in recognition as they flew off. (If you're not familiar with the British slang, extract digit means, "Take your finger out of your ass".

That afternoon they dropped containers of food by parachute, which included chutney, of all things. The food was not designed for those of us who had eaten only rice and, sometimes, some vegetables. It was very rich but we ate it anyway.

That evening the Brits from compound #6 gave us all a treat to eat ....STEAK! They had slaughtered a bull and cooked the meat... no aging. Naturally, we had rice and some of the food and spices that had been parachuted. The taste of the meat was the answer to our dreams as far as food was concerned. We chewed and swallowed until our stomachs were full. That night, my teeth, gums, and jaws started to ache from all the chewing. We were so excited, we couldn't sleep.

May 1ˢᵗ

I felt so upset today, I don't know Karnik dear, but that was some strong and deep feeling that I can't describe when Mrs. Paul called me on the phone to tell me that some prisoners were liberated in Burma. We are hoping to God that you boys are in the liberated group. After her telephone call I was sort of in a dream world, a dazed state of mind...that poor mind of mine wandering in far, far lands with an effort, quite superhuman, to search for traces of my darling. Sweetheart, call it whatever you want, but I have a real mother's intuition, presentiment, a strong feeling that I am going to hear from you soon.

Good God, make this humble, legitimate wish of mine come through. Come on sweetheart, pop up from your unknown place.

May 2, 1945: Everyone woke up complaining of aching and painful jaws, teeth, and gums. That was one kind of pain with which we were all happy to with. We hadn't eaten anything which required any heavy chewing for six months, and for many it had been one, two, or three years.

Later that evening, after we had eaten and were walking around the large entranceway, we heard a hard knock at the front prison door. One of the men opened the door cautiously while another held a cocked rifle. In walked a large man who spoke English. He wore olive drab fatigues, an Aussie-type hat, and black boots. He identified himself as a British war correspondent. Others heard the commotion, gathered around him, and touched him, asking a million questions. I couldn't get my eyes off of him. He was about six foot three, with black curly hair, and he looked so healthy with his unusual rosy cheeks. As I looked past him at the faces of my buddies, I was shocked at the realization of what sickly, pale skeletons we all were. We had all acquired a prison pallor at the same time, and we'd never noticed the slow changes. There were no mirrors to monitor the visual changes. Spellbound by the presence of this magnificent correspondent, we listened as he spoke. He told us his name, but after all these years it has faded from my memory.

May 2nd

Will this day start a beginning of good luck for us?

Mrs. Paul called me again this morning to tell me that her son Chester, Lt. Paul has been FOUND among the liberated group of the Burma POWs.

Oh Karnik, of course this is not the real good news for me and Pop, but I hope so, so strongly that it is the forerunner of your good news for us.

I am so glad for Mrs. Paul. She felt sort of self-conscious to tell me about her sons' safety, but she decided (she told me) to call me up and break the news because she said that helps me to hope for your safety more strongly.

Oh darling, I hope, I pray that you too are also among the liberated lucky boys.

My hope is so strong, so realistic...you will laugh at me, but I feel like turning everything upside down and find you out because <u>I know, I feel</u> *that there is some news in the air from you. I feel like putting a chair next to our door and get the news by mail, telegram, or somehow as soon as possible.*

Come on my Darling! Put an end to this crucifying suffering.

The correspondent told us that the Gurkha Riflemen had just parachuted near us and would be heading here to the prison within a few hours. I had never met a Gurkha face-to-face but had heard a lot about their history and exploits. The Gurkha soldiers from Nepal had served in the British and Indian armies since 1816. These elite infantrymen left their native land to enlist in military service and go wherever the British had need of them. After retirement, they returned to their native Nepal to enjoy their pensions.

The character of these soldiers is best described by the following short anecdotes: During World War II, the Japanese overran a British supply dump in Burma, and the Gurkha Guard detachment at the supply dump was reported missing. A week later, the seven Gurkha riflemen, the missing detachment, reached the British lines, after they had fought their way through the Japanese lines and thick jungles, carrying the unit's money chest all the way.

A captured member of the 1st Battalion, 7th Gurkha Rifles, escaped from a Japanese POW Camp in Southern Burma and walked 600 miles in five months, finally reaching his lines.

A Bren gunner of the 4th Gurkha Rifles sank with his weapon during a river crossing. Knowing that he must never lose his weapon, he clung to it until rescuers pried him loose from it and brought him to the surface before he drowned.

Six Gurkhas in Burma in World War II earned the Victoria Cross. One member of the 4th Battalion of the 8th Gurkha Rifles was wounded in a Japanese attack, losing one eye and one hand. He continued to fire his rifle with his left hand for four hours, and later, 31 dead Japs were found in front of his position. These were remarkable soldiers.

Just as the correspondent had told us, the Gurkhas arrived at our prison entrance, and we welcomed them with great joy. They were smiling, showing their bright white teeth. The entranceway was getting crowded so most of the prisoners backed off to let the soldiers have room to sit on the ground and relax. The Brits brought out some food. Now that we had so much rice, we could be generous and share our bounty with them I was very tired, so I returned to my compound to sleep.

May 3, 1945: I woke up at the crack of dawn and helped prepare the breakfast for our compound. We still had some condiments from the food containers that had been parachuted in by the British. All of us gathered what little we had, so that when the time came to leave, we'd be ready.

Later that morning, a gregarious American officer and his aide entered our prison. He offered to send word to our families. A complete list was provided with the help of his aide. I'm sure his intentions were good, but, as I later learned, my parents, like many others, first heard about us through the newspapers. Word came to us that the tender had arrived at the Rangoon docks and was ready for us to board her for the short trip to the British hospital ship anchored at the mouth of the Rangoon River. Gathering our few mementos, we looked, one last time, at the source of our pain and suffering. If only Vern and the others had made it, we could have all left for home together. What a waste of American lives because of bad judgement by our commander Colonel William H. Blanchard.

I shall never forgive him or forget him!

OUR LIBERATION DAY– MAY 3, 1945

Thank God for our liberation! We had all regarded our Easter lily as a symbol of promise for our liberation, ...and in five weeks we were free!

By this time, we were high-spirited, strutting down the streets of Rangoon, heading for the docks, which were about six city blocks away. I had my galvanized tin pan from which I had eaten, and the black bowl from which I had drunk, along with the carved utensils which I sometimes used. I used a pair of chopsticks more frequently, which I had found on the rafters of compound #8. I also kept the Japanese rifle, the ivory cigarette holder I found in the Japanese quarters, and my trusted leather jacket, which has remained a very special memento of mine. Wearing it during many of my beatings probably saved me from having broken bones instead of just bruises. I had searched my area and couldn't find the shaving knife I had fashioned out of a piece of a barrel hoop. Even now, I miss that most of all, because it kept my mind and hands busy and made me feel useful.

On reaching the dock, we boarded the tender and waited anxiously to proceed down the river to the Bay of Bengal, where the *HMHS* (His Majesty's Hospital Ship) *Karapara* was anchored. All were aboard and ready to cast off when a small group of Ghurkas came running towards us, waving and shouting for us to wait. They were shoving a Japanese soldier, whom they had caught, ahead of them. His head was bandaged and, as he came closer, we saw the fear in his eyes. It was then that we saw a box that was being held between two Ghurkas. They boarded the tender, and put the Japanese soldier in the brig on the first deck. The box was opened, and we saw to our horror what the Ghurkas had done. It was full of bloody ears. The Ghurkas had caught a bunch of Japanese and kept this one alive to verify that they were Japanese ears. I could not believe my eyes. With all the suffering and beatings which I had gone through, I knew that I could never have done that to any man. I am at peace with myself in that my experience enhanced my compassion for mankind and my intolerance of man's inhumanity to man.

The Ghurkas left. We headed downriver, soon arriving at the hospital ship. As we lined up and then climbed up the ramp to the first deck, we were greeted by the captain and crew. After they set us up on the large deck, each of us was given a blanket and then ordered to the showers, where we stripped down and were deloused. After showering, we threw our loincloths and any other leftover clothing through the portholes into the bay. I was able to squirrel away my leather jacket on the deck under my blanket. We were all given pajamas and some good food and drink. After we lay on the deck talking about a host of things on our minds, we wondered how our buddies were doing on the march....had they been killed? Had any survived the march? There was nothing we could do

but wait and wonder. Soon, we fell into a well-deserved sleep under our
blankets.

May 4^{*th*}

Good morning! It is quite strange for me to start with a "Good morning", but
I felt like telling it to you my precious Karnik. Are you well? Liberated? I pray
that God gives us that super happiness to know that you are alive and well. I
don't expect as yet to hear from you personally, but any news giving us the
assurance that you are O.K. will satisfy us. I will be patient to let happiness
come to us bit by bit. The minute that we will be told of your liberation (now I
realize that you are a POW) you will be reborn to us again. Oh darling, just
imagine of the
happiness of your parents! Just the thought of it makes me feel weak, of an
anticipated happiness.
You are everybody's darling. Mrs. Exerjian, the Balakians feel about you as if
you were their own Karnik. Verjin is going to have me over her house for a
weekend as soon as we get the "good news"! Do you believe in dreams? Well
if you do, we can be sure that happiness is coming to us. Specially Daisy's few
dreams are so impressive and of a happy foreboding nature. Everyone's dreams
were so hopeful about you. I must admit that at times they are helping me to
believe in their particular meaning.
We are going to see the Paul's this Sunday. They invited us for dinner. I hope
by Sunday another happy mother too! It is going to be quite hard for me to
smile and show happiness for Mrs. Paul while my darling remains still missing.
Tell me what day will be the happiest day of my life?
Of course darling, I had many happy days in my life, and it is unfair to think that
I didn't have any happy days. However, that day, the day I'll hear from you or
of you, will be the most happy day of my life.

May 4, 1945: We woke up the next morning, had a delicious breakfast
with real eggs and bacon, pancakes with lots of syrup and butter, juice,
coffee, and buns. My taste buds thanked me. Afterwards, those of us
who needed new dressings on our sores or wounds visited the ship's sick
bay. The *Karapara* arrived at the docks in Calcutta about mid-morning.

An announcement came over the loudspeaker, laying out the protocol for disembarking. Guns and other trophies were to be left aboard ship. The British complied, but the Americans immediately devised ways to sneak the few rifles off the ship. I quickly dismantled the Japanese rifle and wrapped it in one of the blankets they had given each of us. The time came when I had to file past the ship's captain and salute, then turn and walk down the gangway and onto the dock. I had wrapped the rifle, disguising it perfectly. I threw my salute, and off the ship I went with my bag of goodies. I wasn't about to give up my souvenirs to a British trophy room.

The greeting on the dock was one big, happy confusion with everyone milling in different directions, smiling and hugging one another. The nurses from our base in Chakulia had come to greet us. They told us that our bomb group had left for Tinian earlier in the year. Soon, they loaded us on busses and took us to the 142nd General Hospital in Calcutta.

142nd GENERAL HOSPITAL IN CALCUTTA

When we reached the hospital, we were directed to our quarters in one of the many wards with rows of hospital cots, very clean and bright in appearance. We were on a robust high, enjoying anything that came our way. Our medical evaluation took priority. We were checked from head to toe. When the doctor examined the skin ulcers on my ankles, I winced in pain. The nurse applied sulphur to the wounds; in a matter of four days, the excoriations had filled in and were starting to heal. All I had needed was some sulphur powder in prison, and those sores would not have festered.

It was time for our first meal at the hospital–a great lunch with all the milk we wanted–meat, ham, and mashed potatoes. How unbelievable to see everyone eating everything in sight, yet being careful not to overdo. There were large bowl on each table with vitamin pills, which we gobbled up like candy. Then came dessert–ice cream–rich, smooth ice cream. We bathed it in chocolate syrup. It was wonderful! We were in paradise! We were cautioned at first not to overeat because our stomachs had shrunk and our digestive system needed time to get back to a normal eating pattern...which they did within a week or two.

After lunch, we went back to our bunks and rested. We visited with one another and exchanged stories. After a few days of this pampering, we were quite comfortable in our living quarters. We got into the routine of waking up, doing our toiletries, going to breakfast, having our wounds redressed, writing letters, generally horsing around, having lunch, visiting with each other, wondering when we would be well enough to be sent home, having dinner and listening to the war news, playing cards, and finally, going to bed.

May 6: The men who had gone on the march finally arrived at the hospital. We were so excited to see our buddies reasonably safe and sound. Burt Parmalee and I happily greeted Brooks, Chet, Norm, and McGivern. Then we had a surprise visit form Major General George Stratmeyer. He came to the hospital especially to greet us. It was an honor to shake his hand.

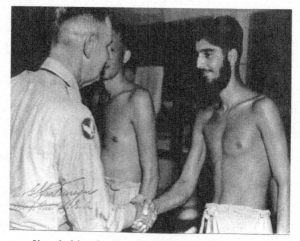

I'm shaking hands with Major General George
Stratmeyer at our hospital in Calcutta.

May 6th, Sunday Evening.

Darling, I can't control any more my impatience and my anxiety about you. So far three of your crew members have been found. Chester Paul, Norman Larsen and Richard Brooks. This morning, in the N. Y. Tribune, I read first about the Larsen boy. Pop and I rushed to the telephone and called Mrs. Larsen and gave her the news. She didn't know anything about her sons' liberation. You can imagine her happiness...I am so glad for her. Any mother suffering as much as I do deserves that happiness. I shall never forget these few last days of my life. I have a very strong, very sure feeling that I am going to hear from you. Each time the door rings my heart pumps up! I can't wait till the next morning to get the paper...I get jumpy at each telephone call. At night I anticipate hopefully the happy hour that I will hear from you. I can't stop my tears of happiness...yes darling, I am so sure you are safe too. Can I hope for a happy Mother's Day? Well, believe me that will be a blissfully memorable day. I can't wait until tomorrow morning. Can you imagine your Mom and Pop reading of our Darling's liberation in the paper? Yes Karnik, after all that happened to many lucky Moms and Pops, maybe we are next on the line. I'll pray, pray and hope till morning!

Pop and I went to the Pauls' today for dinner. Vernon Henning's sister came with us too. What a change I noticed on Mrs. Paul's face and expression. She looked to me at least fifteen years younger! She was so happy, so thrilled over the wonderful news. Indeed, the whole family was jubilant. Chester's wife, Shirley, was there too. She looked like a bright young girl. They all feel so sure that the next good news will come from you. Come on Darling, don't disappoint us. Au Revoir for tomorrow!

May 7: The Chinese POWs who were on the march also entered the hospital for treatment. I'd decided to visit their ward and search out the little Chinese soldier who'd doled out the rice when we were in solitary. He was kind to us even though the Japanese guard was always watching him as he scooped the rice into our pans. If the guard was distracted, he'd slip us an extra scoop. He'd risked a lot in doing so, but he had never gotten caught. I wanted to thank him for helping us when he could. Through an interpreter, I was able to find him. When I met the Chinese soldier, I hugged him. He smiled, as he always did. He could not speak English, and I could not speak Chinese, but somehow we connected. One of the Chinese men interpreted for us. He told me, "Your friend's name is Long Dsong Heow."

I gave him my name in return.

The interpreter continued, "Heow would like to know if you could write a letter to his father in Chungking, telling him that his son is safe and not to worry."

"Of course I will do it," I said, and carried out the task the following day. Heow approached me with a coin in the palm of his hand.

The interpreter said, "He told me that he will break the coin in half, and he will keep one and you will keep the other, and when you meet again, you will join them together."

I did not know what to say. I gave him a big hug, and the interpreter wrote Heow's address on a piece of paper.

The Chinese troops left the 142nd General Hospital in Calcutta a few days before we did. I said good-bye to Heow and promised to write to his father in Hunan, China.

After I got home in June 1945, I wrote a letter to Heow thinking that he would have been home by that time. I got a letter back in Chinese. I found someone to translate it for me. In his letter, he stated that it was the first time in six years that he had had any news about his son. He thanked me profusely and asked me to please forward the accompanying letter that he had written to his son. I wrote back that I would and he wrote back again to please try to find out where he could be. These letters covered a period from June 1945 to May of 1946.

I wrote letters in May, June, and July of 1946 to the 142nd General Hospital in Calcutta, India, and also to the Adjutant General's Office in St. Louis, Missouri. The Hospital was closed and the records were en route to the States. Ultimately, I was never able to get any information about Heow except that the Chinese were on their way back to China...on foot. Could not our government have spared a C-47 and flown them to China? To this day I have no idea of his whereabouts.

May 7th 1945

VE Eve for Europe!

This is a memorable day for many, many millions in Europe and all over the Allied world. Oh my darling, will tomorrow be my own victory day too? My expectation is so strong that it terrifies me when I think of the immense relaxation I will feel when I hear the news of your liberation. I was half crazy all day today. I bought several papers with the hope of seeing your liberation news. In one article, from a Calcutta correspondent, I read a paragraph that had only a partial list of the Americans freed from Rangoon. I pray and pray, and hope so hard, so fervently that our darlings' name be included in that delayed list of names. Hope and courage...I am using up to an extreme extent these two life giving elements. I am in such a state of super tension that my throat chocked all day long, and I had moist eyes many, many times during the day.

Albert Elby is liberated and home from Europe. I didn't see him yet. Now it is your turn to get liberated and be home soon.

Your Pop is very, very nervous too. You know he is not so talkative but the strain of such acute feelings is plainly visible on his face. Grandma is the most calm among the three of us. I have no right to judge from appearances, but my actual experiences taught me that a Mother's feelings cannot be surpassed by anyone else's! Darling, don't laugh at me if I tell you confidentially, that I am sure the day I hear from you I imagine I am going to cry all day! Tears of supreme happiness will do me good. It's good to cry once in a while, and when you cry for a happy happening, tears are most soothing and quite welcome.

I want to be a happy Mother too an this Mother's Day. I know you won't disappoint me! All our friends are so anxious to hear from you! Daisy saw your name on the liberated list...in her dream. That little girl had strange dreams about you. She couldn't have liked you any better if you were her brother or cousin. I imagine how she will be tremendously happy too, the minute we get news from you.

If that happens during the day, I'll call Pop, then the Jeffersons. Now the funny part is that everybody insists on getting the news first. Well, I won't mind sitting *by the phone and telling all our friends that our only darling has been reborn to us. Only I am afraid I'll choke or break down with each call. Well, God will send me a good provision of strength and calmness to do this most pleasant duty of informing our friends.*

I received two letters from Mrs. Henning, and Leon McCutcheon's wife. They both know you and like you very much. They too, have no news from their boys. Well, next is our turn...Yippie!!!

May 8, 1945: VE Day (Victory in Europe...at last!!!) Now we must push for VJ Day (Victory over Japan!). We were all so happy that the war in Europe was over. At last, Hitler was destroyed along with all his Nazi regime. This was the topic for days.

May 8th ...EUROPEAN VE DAY!

This was another day of deep meditation for me. Oh, Karnik, I know some day, pretty soon, you will read these lines, that's why I don't want to make them so deep or so very impressive for you. I know, my poor innocent boy, you too are suffering immensely because of this miserable war. Europe is rejoicing its legitimate reward. A peace with an unconditional surrender from the German Beasts #1. I wonder if there is any family left without a permanent sorrow to endure. Will this war be the last one on this world? I went to the church this evening for a service of thanksgiving for the end of the European war. Who said Americans are not sensible, the city was very far to represent an atmosphere of rejoicement. How can one rejoice over so much unhappiness that the Germans spread all over Europe? All day long I was in a dizzy state of mind. I went to the stationery store early this morning, 7 A.M., to get the papers. It seems to me that God wants to test my courage once more before granting me the happiest moment in my life!

Mrs. Larsen, and Mrs. Paul telephoned. They too are anxious for us, but my hope is great and solid more than ever! My nerves are getting very shaky. Darling, do you blame me? During these last almost 6 months, I suffered very, very deeply, and I tried hard to keep a calm and sort of a smiling face for my family and also my friends.

Lt. McGivern is also liberated, in fact Mrs. Paul told me that her son, Chester, McGivern and Brooks are on their way home. I pray to God to make my boy next to start on his way home. I am afraid that my courage is deserting me. Please pray hard with all your precious, darling heart that God puts an end to our suffering. This state of mind and soul is something that crushes us without mercy. Tomorrow, first thing, I'll rush out to get the morning papers. Who knows, my Victory day has yet to come. Maybe tomorrow will be your parents' happiest day.

May 10: Chet Paul told me that he'd sent a short message to his wife, Shirley, saying that we were well. She'd probably called my folks. Mother's Day was close at hand. I wished I could be home on that day, but it wasn't possible. We were getting stronger, though, and my sores were healing. The pressure and anxiety we had over leaving for home was at maximum level.

May 10th 9:30 AM

Darling, how long will last this torture? Yesterday was another day of tense, very tense feelings and nervous expectation. Mrs. Paul telephoned this morning. I told her that there was no news from you. Then she told me that Shirley, Chesters wife, received a telegram this morning from Chester telling her just these 2 words. "ALL WELL AND SAFE". Now, what does that mean? I am nearly breaking my poor brain, but I really can't give an exact definition of his telegram. Mrs. Paul called Washington to ask if there is any other news from the other boys. They told her, "not yet", and that they will notify us as soon as they get our boy's names. But she told me again, and again that the telegram said, "ALL WELL AND SAFE". After all, I imagine that Chester knows what he is cabling. His folks know that he is well and safe, so why should he use the words, "ALL WELL", instead of I AM WELL, or EVERYTHING IS WELL, and also why mention the word "SAFE", we all know that he is safe all right? Did he want to inform us that all the boys of his crew are safe and well? You see darling what crucifying thoughts are our constant companions.

Since last Wednesday, Pop and I are suffering so miserably. I am expecting news, something from morning till evening. I expect each minute to come, so full of something from you. I expect the door bell to ring any minute   Last night, I was almost going to faint. We had company, Mr. Kurkjian (Vahanigs Grand

Pa), Rev. Simonian and Uncle Harry. All of a sudden, the door bell rang very insistently....Karnik, I felt something that I can't describe to you. I thought it was my telegram, but it was a mean false alarm. Believe me, sweetheart, my heart started to beat so fast and irregular that I thought I was fainting.

Pop rushed to get the papers this morning...still nothing in them this morning, but I can still hope for today, you know, I can hear from Washington, from Nona through the New York Times, or through Shirley because her father works for the N.Y. Tribune. I also expect to hear from YOU! Oh boy, I'll get hilarious to receive a piece of paper signed with your name on the bottom. Believe me darling, that miraculous piece of paper will be my life saver, worth all and any kind of money and happiness put together. Am I expecting too much? I'll write this evening again.

May 11: I sent a telegram home for Mother's Day telling my family that I was O.K. and coming home soon.

May 11ᵗʰ

Mother's Day is around the corner, is your great good news on it's way to your Mom and Pop? Oh darling, my heart beats fast, sort of exuberant and exalted at the thought that I may be liberated from this horrible agony of over 5 months! I have been through days that I thought I was getting insane. Oh darling, why do I love you so deeply? I <u>over love you</u>, why? Because you are my own son? Of course because of that...but also and especially because you grew up to be such a wonderful, kind, and perfect young man that not only your parents love and cherish you, but believe me darling, you are everybody's darling at home. You are the thought and talk of the town. I know all our friends are anxious to hear from you.

I went to the A.G.B.U. sewing center yesterday to get some wool to crochet for our poor compatriots. Well darling, you should have seen all the ladies present, they were so excited, so hopeful, so happy that your good news will come too. Everybody was smiling for me. One lady came to me, Mrs. Sahagian, and she told me not to worry at all. I have never seen her so happy. "I have opened cards for you." she said. "Your boy is <u>safe</u>, believe my word, <u>safe</u>, and he will be home soon." she said. That happy determination on her face did impress me, she was almost jubilant when she said that. I have moments that I BELIEVE YOU ARE

SAFE TOO! Please darling, keep on praying with me for all of us to be happy again. I don't want money, I don't want fame, I don't want the impossible. All I pray for and want is to own again the precious possession that our good God gave us 21 years ago. I want my only precious boy to come back to me. Darling, not only back to your parents, but a fine boy like you can serve as a leading example for other boys of your generation. I know you can do much good for mankind!

Grandma told me that we will hear from you this weekend. Today is Friday, the beginning of the weekend. I hope so much that her guess materializes. I already read the morning papers, but nothing yet to let loose my happiness. But who can tell, I may receive a telegram or some news from the Times and Tribune corespondents' offices or a miraculous cable from you. I can't wait any longer sweetheart. Can't you see the intense suffering on your Mom?

May 12th 1945 Saturday 2:00 AM after midnight.
THANKS GOD! YOU ARE SAFE AND WELL!

We read about your liberation in the paper and a half an hour later we received your cable. Our house was flooded with friends, laughing and crying with us. The telephone kept on ringing all day and night. I AM A HAPPY MAMA AGAIN! I am too exhausted now to write any details about today. Goodnight my darling, thanks God!

May 13, 1945: Mother's Day. I hoped Mom had gotten the telegram so that she could enjoy Mother's Day. I wished that I could have been there, but soon, I'll be home.

May 13th 1945   Mother's Day

Mother's Day to every mother, but to me it is the happiest day of my life. Oh my darling, my happiness is so great, so wonderful, so apropos for today that I feel and believe that the hand of God was upon us. We are so overjoyed, so thrilled, and above all so thankful to God.

I wish you were here with us to see and enjoy with us the happiness, but I am going to describe the day of happiness of yesterday and this morning's Church Service.

Yesterday morning, as usual went down to get the morning papers. Pop and

I went through both papers, but we were disappointed again. Each disappointment gave us a sore feeling and another coat of torture on our hearts. I had pupils coming in all morning and I had a class-meeting in the afternoon. About 2:00 PM the kids started to come in.

The telephone rang! I went to answer. Mrs. Daglian (Ara's Mother) was calling. She asked me how I was. As usual I said I was waiting for my good news....she hesitated for a moment, then she said, "Sophie, don't get upset, but Ara just called me and told me that he saw your Karnik's name in the paper as a rescued airman." Oh, my darling, I shall never be able to describe what I felt at that moment. I couldn't believe my ears and also was anxious that what Ara read was truly the real good news we were waiting for. I screamed, (high C, I suppose) to the kids to run down and get a N.Y. Telegram. The whole house was electrified... that was the real atmosphere of the house!

They brought up the paper and all 12 pairs of eyes scanned the pages, but in our excitement we all missed the 4-5 lines on the front page that was written about you. I went to call Pop to tell him the super news. Can you believe me Karnik, I forgot your Pop's number so the rest of the excited crowd helped me to get in touch with Pop. I don't know how I talked to Pop...all I was doing was half crying, half laughing, half screaming, and all the kids ran into my room to show me your name in the paper. Karnik, my most precious darling, that was a delirious, happy moment. I, the kids, about 15 of them and Grandma were just half crazy, we were crying, laughing, hugging each other, kissing each other, and in the meantime our telephone starting ringing every other minute, all day long. Friends poured in every minute, Grandma and I shuttled all day long from the door to the telephone..everybody was crying with happiness. You can imagine my supreme emotion of happiness when from the telephone they read me your cable... "Dear Mom"....Those sweet two words ringing in my ears like a wonderful, beautiful happy music...my happiness had no limit from then on.

All the kids were released with one week of "Emergency Vacation". Now I realized that I had a duty to fulfill, notify my friends as soon as possible. I started with the Jeffersons...nobody was home, can you beat that. Nevarte and Daisy made me promise to give them the good news as soon as received, (they were second in line after Arsen) and here I was calling them and nobody home! I kept calling my friends and asking them to call other friends, in the meantime telephones and friends kept on pouring incessantly.

I hardly found a moment to go out for some emergency shopping. I saw Daisy coming my way, so with a broad smile on my face I kept telling Her...YES!! YES!! She was dumbfounded for a second, then she looked at me, (Louise and Suzan were with me at that moment, all happy smiles and kissing me) and all of a sudden she asked... KARNIK? I said YES!!!! Darling, that screaming of happiness, I am sure that everyone on the block heard. Then she started to yell for her mother with all the power of her healthy lungs. (Nevarte was at Annette's apartment across the street.) She came to the window, she was so stunned of happiness, that she was going to jump out of the window. So Daisy dragged me up to tell her all about the lightning like happenings of the afternoon. She openly cried of happiness.

Oh boy, Pop was home when I got home. We kept on kissing each other for about 2-3 minutes, crying and laughing at the same time. Friends kept on coming in all afternoon and evening. The telephone kept us busy without interruption. We had two sets of full house in one evening.

I wrote a letter to you before I went to bed. I did not sleep all night...I was so happy, upset, and had a terrible headache. I had to take the same pills the doctor gave me when I first heard of your bad news...anyway, I didn't sleep all night.

May 16 or 17, 1945: I wrote a letter home telling my family once again, that I was O.K. and not to worry. As the boys received their medical clearances from the hospital, they got a green light to travel, and left a few at a time.

May 23, 1945: Chet, McGivern, and Brooksy got their orders to go home. I was sorry I couldn't join them, but I was excited for them. Chet promised to call my folks and tell them I was O.K. In a few days they would be home. As the days passed, more of the guys were leaving, both Americans and British.

On June 1, 1945: I GOT MY ORDERS TO SHIP HOME. I was given a choice of either going directly home on a C-47 or going to Kashmir to live on a houseboat with servants for a month. Then I would be shipped home by way of troop ships going across the Pacific to San Francisco, and finally by plane to New York. Needless to say, the Kashmir vacation would have been great, but without hesitation, I chose instead to go directly home by plane. I packed the few things I had in a large duffle bag, which included my Japanese rifle and other souvenirs from my prison days.

June 1, 1945: Only three of us were to leave this day at 1900. "Bud" Edwards, Harlan Greene, and I were taken to the airport, checked in, and our baggage was inspected. Nothing was said about my souvenirs. They had given all of us the army wristwatch, which I still have today. Boarding the plane, a C-47, I noticed bucket seats along each side. Along with us, American civilians would be flying. I was a bit apprehensive about flying without a parachute, but the flight crew assured me that I would not need one. We took off for Delhi, went from there to Karachi, and on to Abadan, Persia. From there the plane was re-fueled in Cairo. Continued flying to Tripoli, Lybia, and stayed overnight, then on to Casablanca, Morocco.

At 1330, we flew to the Azores for another overnight, then onto Newfoundland, the last stop before home. Our names were called out every time we boarded the plane to check that no one was missing. When we boarded the plane in the Azores, I noticed that some new faces had joined us in Morocco. A man came over to me and introduced himself. The years have dimmed my memory of his name, but he knew my mother. Remarkably, he was of Armenian descent as was I, and he happened to be the editor of an ethnic newspaper, the ARMENIAN SPECTATOR, for which my mother wrote articles from time to time. He knew that I was missing in action, and was so happy to see that I was O.K. We were on the last leg of our journey, and we talked a bit more. I finally fell asleep. Hours later, I was awakened by the pilot's voice on the loudspeaker. He said that we were approaching LaGuardia Airport in Queens, Long Island. The hours went by so slowly. I looked out the windows, thinking the Atlantic Ocean was endless.

The plane was slowly descending when finally I saw our shoreline in the distance, and visions raced through my mind of my parents and grandmother. How were they? Would they look much older? Had Mom and Dad held up well? I started to get anxious, nervous, as we drew closer. Suddenly I recognized New York City. At that moment, the pilot's voice came over the speaker again.. "Everyone, look out the right-side windows of our plane." As the plane quickly descended, the pilot banked sharply and down to about 800 feet....and there she was – so beautiful...so magnificent...MY Statue of Liberty. The pilot circled around her once more as tears unashamedly filled my eyes and rolled down my face. I was home at last!...Free from the beatings, the starvation, the mental and physical torture, with no word from home, and no Red Cross packages...nothing. God bless America, MY land of the free. In all my prayers, I had asked for the strength to survive and return home, and now I was home!

As we disembarked, I had a chance to thank the pilot for what he had done and how much it meant to me. I said good-bye to the editor, and to my buddies, then made my way through Customs.

A bus took a few of us to Fort Dix for separation. The first thing that I noticed was some MPs guarding a group of prisoners who were cleaning trash from the walkways with a broom and dust pan. I saw the letters POW stenciled on the back of their clean fatigues. Some were smoking and drinking a coke. Wow! What a contrast from my imprisonment. The MPs told me they were German POWs. I shook my head in disbelief and checked in at the main desk. I was briefed with the others, and then individually given instructions on my furlough and discharge, or so I thought. However, the soldier interviewing me said that I would get a 60-day furlough, and then I had to report back and put in three more months to qualify for discharge. I was told , for an honorable discharge, I had to have 85 points. I only had 82 points at that time, which was why I had received a furlough instead of a discharge. I was furious and frustrated but what was there to do? This was another example of the numerous nonsensical regulations which the military enforced. What use could I have been? Both wars were over, and there was nothing for me to do. I complied...utter stupidity!

After receiving my orders regarding when and where I should report back, I was bussed to New York City. Quickly, I hopped onto the IRT subway, headed for Washington Heights, and exited at the 190th Street Station. Walking through the turnstiles, the filtering of sounds and smells, the elevator construction, I became excited by the familiarity of it. On reaching ground level, I walked out of the arcade and onto the street. I could barely believe my eyes. Everything was exactly as it had been when I left.

Aware of the shock my family might suffer at their first sight of me, I stopped at the corner ice cream parlor and used the pay phone to call upstairs to my home in that same apartment building. Grandma answered and it was unbelievable to hear her loving voice, a balm to my battle-worn soul. When I told her that I was downstairs, and that I'd be on my up immediately, she explained to me that Mom was at the grocer's, but would be right back at any moment. I hung up, rounded the corner into my apartment building (601 West 190th Street), ran into the elevator, and got off on the sixth floor. My heart was pounding with emotion. Grandma was standing inside the open door. I rushed to her, hugged her, kissed her–thought I'd never let her go.

Someone must have seen me and rushed to the grocery store with news of my arrival, or Mom had an intuition that I was already home. Her feet came flying through the door that we'd left open in our haste, and, at last, she was within my reach. Neither of us spoke. Instead, we let our tears speak for us. Grasping at one another, we cried for an endless interval, afraid to let go.

When we called Pop, he wasted no time in leaving the office to come directly home. And when he walked through the door, realizing that, finally, his family was whole again, we stood in time like old strangers, not knowing whether this vision was real, or whether our hard hopes had produced some kind of fictional illusion. Too exhausted to shed any more tears, we clasped hands in a handshake that I will never forget—one that simultaneously congratulated me on my manhood and expressed his love and admiration for me. Then we embraced long and hard.

Daisy Jefferson, the daughter of our dear family friends, was there with a few of my mother's piano students. Daisy and her family had helped my mother to keep her hopes up, so it was right that she was there. The rest of the afternoon was filled with friends and phone calls. My parents did not press me for any details of my captivity. There would be plenty of time later. I did, however, tell them of the loss of my crew members. That night, I had my first meal at home and went to sleep in my old bed, thinking how perfect it could have been if my buddies had made it back, too.

The next morning, as I went for a walk around the neighborhood, a Spalding rubber ball came bouncing towards me. I instinctively grabbed it. A kid about twelve years old rushed up to me with an oversized glove on one hand and with a baseball cap off to the side of his head, said, "Gimme da ball, or I'll waltz one up your snot box ."

I laughed, gave him the ball, and went on my way.

I was home!

Epilogue

During my 60-day furlough, I visited friends and phoned my crew—especially the families of my buddies who did not return. That was the hardest part of all, particularly the folks of Vernon, who had been my closest buddy. Now sixty years later there are three of us left of the six that survived; Chet Paul, Norman Larsen, and me. Richard Brooks died in late 2003. He lived alone in California. My postcard to him was returned with a handwritten "Deceased" on it, I knew he was gone. I called Chet and Norman with the sad news. In 1945 there were one hundred and fifty Americans. Now fifty-nine years later there are thirty-two left.

The best thing the government had given us was the G.I. Bill of Rights. It helped immensely in returning our country to its feet with educated veterans that invigorated the business world. For four years I studied art

–drawing and illustration– at the Art Students League in New York City. After having seen an ad for an illustrator's position for six months in Pittsburgh, Pennsylvania, I decided to try for it. The owner of the studio liked my work, and he hired me at $125 per week.

The most fortuitous thing about working in Pittsburgh was that I met a young woman, Diana Kutchukian, and before the year was up we were married in Pittsburgh on November 29, 1952. She was a beautiful person both inside and out. I returned to New York to study graphic design and gain experience in layout and typography. During the next five years, I was hired and fired by small agencies until I finally got my big break at Grey Advertising. I stayed with Grey for eleven years, during which time I became a Group Head Art Director. After leaving Grey, I became an art director for new Colgate products at Ted Bates, for three years until I became disenchanted. I knew Gaylord Adams since we lived in the same town. He had said to me, "If you ever want to leave Ted Bates, give me a call". I wanted a change so I called and he and his partner Don Flock and I hit it off. I joined Gaylord Adams, Don Flock & Associates, a packaging design and corporate identity firm in New York. I became an account executive, handling and getting new accounts, and I also did some photography and design. It was by far my most exciting and fulfilling professional experience due mostly because of the people I worked with. We worked hard at the firm and played hard on the racket ball courts. After seventeen years, I retired. I now live with my wife in the beautiful town of River Edge, New Jersey. We have two daughters -- Karla, who married David Robertson; and Linda, who adopted our most wonderful granddaughter, Alicia, from Guatemala and is engaged to be married.

Although my POW experience was a miserable one with lingering memories, it was also an awakening one, which made me aware of my fortitude under adversity. Until that time, I had been a shy kid, but the military and the time I spent as a prisoner of the Japanese, brought me out of my shell and into the real world. I now have a healthy self-respect because of what I survived.

As I parachuted from our plane, I watched it spin down to the ground in flames. The realization that my friends had perished, along with my best friend, in one large explosion affects me adversely even now.

Most of my POW comrades have had others ask, "What was it like? Was it rough.? Did they beat you? What did they feed you?"

A POW will bypass these questions in a sentence or two because we realize that as civilians they have no experience in these areas. How can they possibly understand what we endured? Most of them are ten to fifteen years younger than we, and they've had no wartime combat experiences. It sometimes happens at parties, if the subject comes up, or in a car pool going to work. Some will talk about how they goofed off during the war, others tell of the cushy jobs they had. I soon realized that they would never comprehend what I went through – not because they were insensitive, but simply because they were inexperienced.

I see now how intolerant I was of those who did not meet with my expectations. But with the help of intensive therapy for POWs, administered through the Veterans Administration, my reactions are more focused. My friends have recognized me as a fun-loving guy without hangups. How could I expect them to know my dark side, when I didn't even know or understand myself. After retirement I had time to think about it? Slowly, as the responsibilities of marriage and fatherhood, and a demanding career in advertising began to wane, my hidden demons emerged. I joined the American Ex-Prisoners of War Organization, and met others in similar situations. My post traumatic-stress disorder (PTSD) was in full bloom, and I was treated for it by VA psycho therapists. Besides the one on one sessions we had small group sessions of five or six POWs. In one of the group sessions that I remember so well is when I first sat in with them and they asked me what was bothering me. I began to tell them of the loss of my close buddy Vernon, who didn't make it out of the plane. I never could understand why I couldn't find a way to help my buddies. Vern's feet were on my shoulders and I had to jump to get out of the way. I always thought that there must have been something that I could have done. One of the other men who had a similar experience asked me a question. He said, "It took you about five to seven minutes to tell us your story. How long do you think it was from the time of the blast to when you had to bale out?" I thought for a bit and said, "Maybe five minutes or so". He said, "Think again...try two minutes...try one minute or less...don't you understand, there was no time, you reacted instinctively. The plane was going down. After you were out you watched the plane and you saw how quickly it went don and exploded." All he said was true and it helped a great deal but I still have moments when it all comes back.

Proper therapy took time, but the benefit of having peace of mind was well worth the effort. My mother had warned my wife-to-be about my sudden flare-ups and unwarranted anger. The wives of ex-POWs are saints to have the ability to manage us. Diana is my guardian angel. She absorbs my dark moods by showing support and by participating in my PTSD sessions. It sounds like all anyone has to do is put in time, but I know it's not that easy. We have worked hard together in sessions. I've become more adept at dealing with issues of self- control, and Diana has learned to exercise patience and understanding. Her inner strength has proven equal to that of any POW alive today. She is a deep thinker, sensitive, caring, a loving wife and my best friend.

Along with other POWs, I currently speak at schools in New Jersey. It's both frustrating and gratifying to see that the majority of listeners are captivated by our stories but, at the same time, know next to nothing about World War II.   When we relate our personal experiences, we end with the message of appreciation for the freedoms we all enjoy in this liberated land and our responsibility as Americans to respect and protect those freedoms. We remind students and adults alike of their singular right to vote, to enjoy each patriotic act offered to them. We also make sure they understand that freedom of speech without responsibility to their spoken word is nothing short of cowardice.

Sooner or later, a student will ask how many men I have killed. I say I don't know because I fought in the air in a B-29 that flew at 20,000 feet, dropping bombs. And I'm glad I don't know. Enemy fighters were shot down, but the pilots of those planes might have escaped before crashing. Maybe some were saved. Maybe not. I don't speculate about it anymore. Killing the enemy is part of what a combat soldier is trained to do. I'm not proud, that in order to survive, I had to kill indiscriminately, without thought to another human being–his ideals, his preferences, his life, or his family ties.   A combat soldier must kill or be killed.   It's as simple as that. And as complicated. In a perfect world, there would be no war, but as history has demonstrated, we live in an imperfect world.

My dear friend and Vietnam veteran, Mark Del Maestro, has answered the "killing question" in the following way:

The truth is that most veterans don't know how many they killed. If they were dropping bombs from planes, or sending missiles, or shooting salvos from navel ships, or firing from army gun batteries, or even shooting their hand weapons, they really don't know. But if a veteran has a number, in most cases he will not share that with you because that is the price of freedom that he must carry with him. If his number is higher than another veteran, it doesn't mean he is a better defender of the USA. It only means that his opportunities were different.

If you could ask a terrorist, "How many people did you kill?" they would be happy to tell you because that is what they do. They blow up planes, busses, and buildings, and themselves, and the people they kill have no idea they are about to die. When our armed forces go after an enemy, they know we're coming. There are no terrorists wearing the uniform of the American armed forces...there are none!"

We were trained to kill when necessary. We were trained to take prisoners...honorably. We were trained to survive. We were trained to bring as much firepower to the battlefield as we could in hope that an enemy would choose to surrender rather than to die. Every veteran who ever served our country never failed in achieving our number one mission...to protect and preserve our freedom, liberty, and way of life for all Americans. We have never failed in doing that.

So don't remember us by how many people we have killed. Please, instead, remember us by how many people we have saved.

Mark Del Maestro
Vietnam Veteran (River Rat)

I have been a member of the American Ex-Prisoners of War, New Jersey Chapter One, since 1983. I became a vice commander and later decided to edit a chapter newsletter for a few years, which provided a platform for us to voice our concerns about the VA healthcare system and for keeping our members aware of their rights for compensation. After a few years, I was given accreditation, along with eight others to become National Service Officer (NSO). As an NSO, I volunteer my services to all combat veterans, particularly POWs in helping them to file claims for disability compensation. For me, it is a way of putting our slogan– 'We help those who cannot help themselves'–into practice. It's very gratifying to be able to repay the efforts of veterans who once helped me. I feel fulfilled whenever I enable a well-deserving veteran to receive his proper disability compensation.

I look back over the years and imagine how wonderful it would have been to have my parents and Diana's parents still alive to enjoy our lives together. They would have loved to see our two daughters grow into fine women, and our lovely granddaughter would have been their pride and joy.

L to R: Karla's husband David Robertson & daughter Karla, my wife Diana, & daughter Linda. May, 2003

Me, my Mother & Father - 1943

Linda's daughter, Alicia. I drew her portrait in charcoal.

During the past few years, I have resumed portrait-drawing. I work from photographs and render in charcoal. My work has been well received, and I currently operate from my web site www.portraitsbykarnig.com for new orders.

My close buddy Vernon
Henning and I in
Clovis, New Mexico.

My father as a member
of Teddy Roosevelt's
Rough Riders.

A fellow POW and friend, Tim Dyes, loaned me a book entitled *Reluctant Odyssey* by Edith Pargeter. Below is a paragraph from that book, with words I'll embrace forever. I will leave you with its sentiment:

"... You take from people, and you give to people, in equal measure. What you receive from one, you give in turn, sometime, somewhere, to another. Very seldom can you return anything to the person who gave it to you. That's the way it is. But you have to bestow it somewhere. It has to flow. It can't be stemmed. It goes on and on, from link to link, the continuity of human wisdom and human affection, too strong to be damned, too stubborn to relent. That's the first and most inexplicable secret of survival. If it stopped, humanity itself would die."

(written in 1945)

Yanks Avenged for Horror Endured in Burma Prison

Former Chicago Sun Reporter Tells of Torture; Aids in Dooming 23 Japanese

By Eddie Doherty

Edward J. Leary, a Chicago Sun reporter until he enlisted in the Army, has come home with the rank of a captain in the Intelligence Section and with as fascinating and terrible a story of spies and prisoners of war and American detective methods as any ever written.

Twenty-three men, Japanese army officers and prison guards who beat and murdered American soldiers, were rounded up by him and placed on trial. Some have been hanged. Others will be hanged soon.

Chicago Nisei Aided.

"I didn't do it all by myself," he said. "I had the help of Tech. Sgt. Harry Suzakawa, a Chicago Nisie. He lives at 4943 Sheridan Rd. and is at present serving as court interpreter in Rangoon.

"Without his aid, and that of other Nisei soldiers, I might still be looking for all the men we wanted. We had descriptions. But all Japs looked alike to me. And all descriptions were alike. 'Five feet four or five, slightly built, course black hair, almond eyes, olive complexion.' Most any Jap would answer that description.

Tarzan Sought First.

"Some of the prisoners had given us a list of names- but had spelled them phonetically, or had given them nicknames such as Tarzan, Moose Face, The Nose, Sparrow, Hollywood, and so forth. We wanted this Tarzan especially, for most of the men said he was particularly vicious.

"We decided to get him if we never got anybody else. But we began with a misapprehension. From his name we deduced he was an enormous fellow; but, checking up on him, we decided that was wrong. We heard he had also been referred to as 'Limpy,' and as 'Wano.'

"There is, of course, no such name as Wano among the Japanese, but, thanks to Suzakawa, we found there was a name that sounded like it. Ueno: there were as many Uenos, however, in the Burma area where we worked, as there were Smiths in America. We rounded them all up and found one who limped. He was Superior Private Koigetsu Ueno.

Confession Obtained.

"He admitted he was a guard in the Rangoon Central Jail, in charge of Cell Block No .5, where American airmen had been held in solitary. He admitted he had been called Tarzan. He also admitted he had beaten every American in his charge until he could lift his baseball bat no more. We were not content with that. We found witnesses who identified him. And Ueno was condemned to hang.

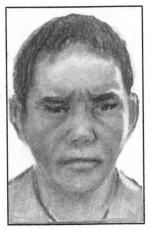

'Tarzan'

"There were three prisons in which brutalities occurred. One was the Rangoon Central Jail, a prison condemned by the British in 1938 as unfit. It had no plumbing. It had few cots if any. It stank. It was cold and dark. Yet the Japs imprisoned 3,000 Allied prisoners there.

All Prisoners Beaten.

"On January 1, 1945 the guards got drunk and beat all American prisoners with clubs. Some of the men died. We heard of a medical officer who refused to treat the victims of clubbings, or to treat the wounded or the sick.

"We learned his identity, Lt. Akio Onishi, and found him without too much trouble. He made a confession, saying that the officer in charge, Capt. Motozo Tazumi, told him to treat American airmen as criminals, not as prisoners of war. We got Tazumi too.

An American Staff Sargent named Montgomery, shot down in a bomber about 50 miles from Rangoon, was one of Onishi's 'patients.' The boy's left hand had been almost severed by flack. It hung by a few threads from his wrist. He was thrown in an open truck, kept at Air Intelligence overnight, questioned, and thrown into jail for a week.

Patient Left on Floor.

"A Japanese doctor cut off the hand, finally, and wrapped the stump of the arm in newspapers. Naturally, the arm became infected.

"Unishi finally condescended to administer an anaesthetic to this boy. When it failed to work the doctor became furious. He belted his patient over the head and left him lying on the floor. American and British prisoners made such a clamor that, at last, a British surgeon was permitted to attend Montgomery - but under Japanese conditions.

"The prisoner was compelled to walk 1,000 feet to a designated spot in the corridor. The surgeon was compelled to work without anaesthetics of any kind. He amputated the arm above the elbow. Montgomery stood the intolerable pain courageously, but when the operation was finished he collapsed. The Japanese insisted he walk back. He could not.

"The other prisoners raised such a howl of indignation that the Japs relented, and let him be carried back to his cell.

"He lay there on the floor for weeks, untended. Surprisingly, he recovered. I guess he was made of iron.

Spy for U,S. Betrayed.

"There was a native of India in the New Law Courts Jail. His name was Ratnun Durai. He was a British subject, but he was employed as a civilian spy by the American Army. He came down, by parachute, to install radios in enemy territory. A former friend betrayed him ----- man later captured and executed by the British.

Capt. Choici Saruta

"Every morning he was taken from his cell and questioned about the radio code our army used. Every morning at 5 o'clock he was brought back to his cell, unconscious. For two months this continued.

"He was beaten with bamboo poles on the inside of his thighs until the skin broke and festered and abscesses formed. He was made to squat, with a bamboo pole beneath his knees, and to keep this position for hours at a time. He was beaten on the back, on the head, and on the arms. But he never talked.

Loyalty Remained Unbroken.

"He was delirious during the last 10 days of his life. But he died with his loyalty unbroken.

"You can imagine then, with what savage emotions I heard Capt. Choici Saruta say, 'Durai was my personal prisoner'!

"The New Law Courts building, a modern office structure, was the Japanese M.P's own jail. There were 10 cells in the concrete storage room at the bottom of the air shaft, cages about 8 feet long by 12 feet wide; yet each cell contained anywhere from 12 to 15 men, and prisoners of war were mingled with lepers, syphilitics, and civilian criminals.

"They could not bathe. They were fed twice a day. There was one sanitary bucket in a cell, and it could be emptied only once a day.

Escape Attempt Blocked.

"American prisoners made an attempt to escape from the jail across the street from the New Law Court annex. They overpowered a couple of guards, took their keys, and let themselves out onto the street. But an alert Japanese sentry kept them from going any farther.

"These men, and their friends, were stripped and beaten steadily for an hour, while the commanding officer looked on, sitting on a table, swinging his legs and smoking cigarettes. Every day for two weeks these men were beaten. Two of them were killed.

"Great soldiers were in these prisons. Among them was an American aviator who refused to bow to the guards as he was supposed to do. He was whacked over the head by every guard in the place, maybe a dozen times a day - yet he was in comparatively good shape when the men were liberated.

New Punishment Devised.

There was another who stole a piece of dried fish. A guard smashed him with a rifle butt. He was made to stand in the sun for hours, with a piece of rotten fish tied to his neck. And every Jap who passed assailed him with a club or fist. He endured it all with admirable fortitude, and lived.

"But the greatest story of all, which I know but vaguely, is that of the British Maj. Seagram, a famous spy who was murdered in the New Law Courts jail after he surrendered.

"The officer had organized a powerful underground movement in Burma. He had interfered seriously with all Japanese operations in the district. He had ambushed raiding parties. He had blown up troop and supply trains.

Native Villages Burned.

"The Japs retaliated by burning native villages and bayoneting every man, woman, and child, who tried to escape.

"They never would have caught Seagram. He surrendered so that no more natives might be burned.

HANDWRITTEN IN PRISON
BY LIONEL HUDSON W/C R.A.F.

This authentic document is a listing of the names of the American prisoners of war who died or were liberated by the British 14th Army from the Rangoon Central Jail, Rangoon, Burma, May 4,1945. *(Please excuse any misspelling of names as the original document was at times difficult to decipher. There are some words and abbreviations that I could not understand but I copied the document as it was originally written.)*

W/C Lionel Hudson kept a log of the men in our compound. He had a small indelible pencil that printed blue on the tissue thin tan paper. It is a remarkable document.

1035

Miller, Donald V. CAPT. 0-660175 - Menomenie, Wisconsin.

1 st Fighter Group, P-51, Pilot.

Bombed supply dump north of Mandalay. Attacked by Oscars, aircraft on fire, bailed out. Walked for three days before contacting friendly Burmese. After 2 days police intervened and handed over to Japs. Held at Memyo for 3 months, got dysentery and no medical attention. On 5/26/44/ taken to Rangoon Central Prison in cell #50 with John Hunt then in solitary for 5 months.

1036

Hunt, John N. CAPT. 0-429047 - McLeansboro, Illinois.

80th Group, P-40, Pilot.

On 12/22/43 was flying escort and my engine cut out over "Hump". Bailed out 15 miles northwest of Taro. Contacted Burmese, making for our lines when captured by Japs. In Memyo for 4 months, then to Rangoon Central Prison on 5/20/44 in cell #50 for three months with Donald Miller and 5 months in solitary.

1037

Ortmeyer, Armin J. CAPT. 0- - Tampa, Florida.

10th Air Force, 459th Squadron, P-38, Pilot.

On 11/27/43 was flying escort to Rangoon. On return was attacked by Oscars, exploded, managed to open chute, badly burned. Captured and taken to City Jail on 11/28/43. Got poor medical treatment, recovered and on 7/27/44 taken to Rangoon Central Prison, compound 5, cell #24. Died in compound 8 on 1/14/45 of beri-beri, malnutrition and bad sores.

1038

Willner, Edward R. 2LT. 0-671824 - Aurora, Illinois.

10th Air Force, 311 Fighter Bomber Group, P-51, Pilot.

On 12/17/43 flew escort to Rangoon. Oscars attacked and caught fire, bailed out west of Rangoon with severe burns. Caught and taken to City Jail on 12/1/43 and got some medical treatment. Taken to Rangoon Central Prison on 7/27/44 cell #15. Had dysentery and little medical treatment.

1039

Gray James M. 1LT. 0- - Philadelphia, Pennsylvania

10th Air Force, 530th Squadron, P-51, Pilot.

On 11/27/43 was flying escort to Rangoon. On return was attacked by Oscars, caught fire, crash landed, severe burns, poor medical treatment. Put into City Jail on 12/1/43. Taken to Rangoon Central Prison 7/27/44. Died 8/14/44 of malnutrition, beri-beri, sores and anemia.

1040

Briggs, Everet E. 2LT. 0- - Raleigh, North Carolina.

10th Air Force, 530th Squadron, P-51, pilot.

On 11/27/43 was flying escort to Rangoon. On return was attacked by Oscars, caught fire, and bailed out, Burmese handed over to Japs and put into City Jail 12/1/43. Transferred to Rangoon Central Prison on 7/27/44 in cell #24. Died 1/27/44 of malnutrition and bad sores.

(No Number - same mission as above 1040)

Angel, Robert F. 1LT. 0- - Richmond, Virginia.

10th Air Force, 530th Squadron, P-51, pilot. On 11/27/43 was flying escort to Rangoon. On return was attacked by Oscars, caught fire, and bailed out, Burmese handed over to Japs and put into City Jail 12/1/43. Died 2/27/44 of dysentery.

1041
Hogan, Dudley W. Jr. 2LT. 0-799184 -Augusta, Georgia.
10th Air Force, 311 Fighter Bomber Group, P-51, Pilot.
On 11/27/43 was flying escort to Rangoon. On return was attacked by Oscars, caught fire, bailed out over GWA bay, after 15 days was captured by Burmese and handed over to Japs. Got medical treatment for slight burns. Entered City Jail on 12/7/43. Transferred to Rangoon Central Prison on 7/27/44 in cell #17.

1042
Wentz, Roy A. 1 LT. 0-654928 - Springfield, Illinois
10th Air Force, 7th Bomb Group, B-24, Navigator.
On 12/1/43 bombed Rangoon, attacked by Oscars, bailed out north of Bassein. Handed over to Japs by Burmese. on 12/9/43 placed in City Jail then transferred to Rangoon Central Prison on 7/27/44. Cellblock 5, cell #11.

1043
Erwin, Grant W. Jr. 1LT. 0-558862 - Milwaukee, Wisconsin.
10th Air Force, 7th Bomb Group, B-24, Navigator.
On 12/1/43 while bombing Ensein we were hit by Ack-Ack and Oscars. Got hit and on fire. Bailed out at 300ft. Out of crew of 10, two known to have bailed out, one injured and unaccounted for. Caught by Burmese at Bassein and handed over to Japs. Taken to City Jail on 1219143, got medical treatment for slight wound and sprains. Transferred to Rangoon Central Prison on 7/27/44 in cellblock 5, cell #18.

1044

Wells, Joseph B. S/SGT. 6934111 - Boone, Iowa.

10th Air Force, 7th Bomb Group, B-24, Gunner.

On 12/1/43 while bombing Ensein we were hit by Ack-Ack and Oscars. Bailed out north of Bassein. Had severe wounds, unable to move. After four days, found by Burmese and handed over to Japs. Got some medical treatment then on 12/9/43 put into City Jail. On 7/27/44 transferred to Rangoon Central Prison, cellblock 5, cell #23.

1045

Rodriquez, Frank S/SGT. - Oakland, California.

Died in prison on 8/27/44.

1046

Hastings, Alvin L. S/SGT. 35357272 - Martinsville, Indiana.

10th Air Force, 7th Bomb Group, B-24, Nose Gunner.

On 12/1/43 while bombing Ensein, attacked by Ack-Ack, Oscars and Tojos for 45 min. Bailed out north of Bassein. Burmese handed us over to Japs. Had sprained ankle, no medical treatment. 12/9/43 taken to City Jail then to Rangoon Central Prison on 7/27/44 in cellblock 5, cell #27.

1047

Farley, Grady M. T/SGT. 14107685 - Russellville, Alabama.

10th Air Force, 7th Bomb Group, B-24, Flight Engineer.

On 12/14/43 we were bombing in northern Burma when patroling Oscars attacked us and we caught fire and had to bail out in the vacinity of Meiktila. Slight burns injury to foot, walked for ten days on "D" rations and one fish. Captured by Burmese and handed over to Japs. Got severe ill treatment and on 12/27/43 was put into City Jail and transferred to Rangoon Central Prison on 7/27/44 in cellblock 5, cell #19.

1048

Johnson, Gostaf (Gus) E. 2LT. 0-682483 - Miami, Florida.

10th Air Force, 7th Bomb Group, B-24, Bombardier.

On 10/26/43 Bombed shipping in Rangoon. Attacked by Oscars, long fight the rammed near coast, had to bail out at low altitude. Walked for six days with no rations. Handed to Japs by Burmese. Ill treatment for four days. Taken to city jail on 11/19/43 and then to Rangoon Central Prison on 7/27/44 in cellblock 5, cell #29.

1049

Bockman, Clifford H. S/SGT. 19075514 - Ione, Washington.

10th Air Force, 7th Bomb Group, B-24, Engineer.

On 12/1/43 he was bombing Ensein when he was attached by Oscars, caught fire, bailed out in jungle north of Bassein, walked for 8 days and contacted Burmese east of GWA. Lived on one "D" ration, one crab and three fish. Handed to Japs by Burmese. Got slight medical treatment for flack wound in leg but he got severe ill treatment at interrogation. Taken to city jail on 12/13/43 and then to Rangoon Central Prison on 7/27/44 in cellblock 5, cell #23

1050

Redd, Charles H. 2LT, 0-669104 - St.Louis, MO.

341 Bomb Group, B-25, Navigator.

On 12/19/43 Bombing Monywa hit ack-ack, bailed out 75 miles Northwest of target, below 500 Ft. Walked twelve days with bombardier 1LT. J. Zizlowski. We were on "D" rations, raw fish and berries. Handed over to the Japanese in sight of our lines. On way to Kalewa we were bound for six days. Even fed I.T. treated until taken 1/17/44 City Jail. Rangoon Central Prison 7/27/44 cellblock 5, cell #17.

1051

Korotkin, Louis 2LT. 0-749567 - Ozone Park, Long Island, N.Y.
80th. Fighter Group, 459 Squadron, P-38
On 2/3/44 Dive Bombing W. Prome. On fire, ack-ack. Bailed out and walked for five days. Fired at elephant, evaded patrols, captured by Japs 2/19/44 and taken to City Jail then to Rangoon Prison 7/27/44, cellblock 5, cell #15.

1052

McClung, Joseph C. SGT. 32288140 - Sheridan Arkansas
373 Squadron, 308 Bomb Group, B-24, Engineer
On 11/27/43 bombing Rangoon Marshalling Yards; engine failure, ack-ack, running fight with Oscars, on fire, bailed out North Bassein. Attacked on the way down, Burmese handed over to Japs. Ill treated at interrogation; fed only once in five days, 12/2/43 City Jail, Rangoon Prison 7/27/44 cellblock 5, cell #19.

1064

Gambale, Gene LT. 0- - Brooklyn, New York.   Bombardier
Bailed out, in City Jail 4/12/44 then to Rangoon Central Prison on 7/27/44. Kicked on mouth trying to escape City Jail, wouldn't eat rice, died of malnutrition 8/1/44.

1065

McKernan, James M. S/SGT. 32281809 - Olcott, New Jersey.
10th Air Force, 9th Bomb Squadron, 7th Bomb Group, B-24, Gunner.
On 4/5/44 L.M.G. killed pilot on low level bomb run Moulmein, Bangkok railways. 7 of crew killed in aircraft, 4 bailed out. Walked two days, then Burmese handed us over to Japs. Taken to City Jail (Rangoon Ritz) on 4/12/44 then on 7/27/44 they placed us in the Rangoon Central Prison in

cellblock 5, cell #22.

1066

Wells, Tyman K. S/SGT. 34478136 - Hattiesburg, Mississippi

9th Bomb Squadron, 7th Bomb Group, B-24, Engineer.

On 4/5/44 L.M.G. killed pilot on low level bomb run at Moulmein, Bangkok railways. 7 of crew killed in aircraft, 4 bailed out. Walked one day, then Burmese handed us over to Japs. En route to Moulmein, train wrecked on bamboo bridge. Taken to the City Jail (Rangoon Ritz) and then to Rangoon Central Prison on 7/27/44 Cellblock 5, cell#19.

1067

Whitescarver, J.T. 2LT. 0-749135 - Pittsburg, Kansas.

459th Squadron, P-38, Pilot.

On 4/2/44 strafed Heho under heavy ack-ack, caught fire, bailed out at 300 ft. and hit,tail of plane with arm and broke it. Survived for 13 days, 120 miles in jungle until Burmese handed me over to Japs in Heho. Wrist rebroken during my interrogation. Mal treated, no medical treatment. Flown to Rangoon (Ritz) City Jail 4/29/44 where we attempted to escape. Rangoon Central Prison on 7/27/44 cellblock 5, cell #28.

1068

Westberg, Wayne R. CAPT. 0- - Moline, Illinois.

12th Bomb Group, 434th Squadron, B-25, Navigator.

On 5/20/44 bombing railways north of Schwebo. Hit by ground fire, had to bail out. Put in Rangoon City Jail on 6/5/44 then moved to Rangoon Central Prison on 7/27/44, cellblock 5, cell 13. Died 8/22/44 of malnutrition, malaria and ill treatment.

Snee, Thomas 2LT. 0-?- New York, New York.

12th Bomb Group, 434th Squadron, B-25, Co-Pilot.

(Same crew as above) Bailed out, not seen again. Japs reported finding his body, chute had not opened.

1069

McCloskey, John H. 1LT. 0-796848 - Pittsburg, Pennsylvania.

434th Squadron, 12th Bomb Group, B-25, Pilot.

On 5/20/44 we were low level bombing north of Shwebo. Hit by ground fire, plane caught fire, had to bail out. Co-Pilots chute failed to open. Sprained ankles and back. Burmese handed him over to Japs. Little medical attention. On 6/6/44 taken to Rangoon City Jail, there were rats. Attempted to escape the "Ritz". He was taken to Rangoon Central Prison on 7/27/44, cellblock 5, cell #13.

1070

Waltrip, Leland, N. S/SGT. 39251831 - Los Angeles, California.

434th Squadron, 12th Bomb Group, B-25, Tail Gunner.

5/20/44 on low level bombing north of Shwebo. Hit by ground fire, plane caught fire, bailed out. Walked for 3 days then Burmese handed me over to Japs near Pinlebu. Ill treated at interrogation with wet raw-hide. On 6/6/44 taken to City Jail where we attempted to escape. On 7/27/44 we were taken to Rangoon Central Prison cellblock 5 cell #28.

1071

Snyder, Norman L. S/SGT. 39828644 - Hawthorne, Nebraska.

434th Squadron, 12th Bomb Group, B-25, Tail Gunner.

On 5/20/44 we were low level bombing north of Shwebo. Hit by ground fire, plane caught fire, had to bail out. Walked for 3 days then Burmese handed me over to Japs near Pinlebu. Had leg burn and got slight medical treatment on 6/6/44 at the "Ritz" City Jail where we attempted to escape. On 71271441we were taken to Rangoon Central Prison cellblock 5, cell #28.

1072
Niland, Edward F. T/SGT. 32251692 - Tonawanda, N.Y.
434th Squadron, 12th Bomb Group, B-25, Radio Operator.
On 5/20/44 we were low level bombing north of Shwebo. Hit by ground fire, plane caught fire, had to bail out. Walked for 4 days then Burmese handed me over to Japs near Pinlebu. Ate Grasshoppers, got some medical treatment for burns on hand and face. On 6/6/44 we were taken to City Jail "Ritz" where we attempted to escape. On 7/27/44 they took us to the Rangoon Central Prison, cellblock 5, cell #15.

1073
Bishop, Louis W. 1LT. 0-702239 - Bensenville, Illinois.
25th Fighter Squadron, 51 st Fighter Group, P-40, Pilot.
On 5/10/44 skip bombed Hsenwi bridge. Plane caught fire from ground fire, had to bail out at 600 feet. Kachins 2 days, got suspicious, left, walked 6 days towards Kunlong along the Nati River, nearly drowned. Captured by Japs at Salween River. Shot at and after interrogation was beaten unconscious. My weight was 220 lbs. On 6/3/44 they put me in Rangoon City Jail (Ritz), where we attempted to escape. Transferred to Rangoon Central Prison on 7127144, cellblock 5, cell #13.

1074
Goodrich, Burdett C. 1LT. 0-750504 - Colfax, Washington.
459th Squadron, P-34, Pilot.
On 6/6/44 was on fire sweep on Meiktela. Attacked by Oscars and forced to land. Walked 4 days with back injured. Met Burmese, then treachery,

shot at followed I killed one and wounded two. Cornered, shot at again 5 pellets. Handed to Japs at Pauk and got medical treatment. On 6/20/44 put into Rangoon City Jail, then on 7/27/44 was transferred to Rangoon Central Prison, cellblock 5, cell #23. Died on 2/24/45 in prison of dysentery and beri-beri.

1075

DuBose, Allen B. Capt. 0-663702 - San Antonio, Texas.
530th Fighter Bomber Squadron, 311th Gp., P-51, Pilot.
On 12/1/43 escort mission to Rangoon when attacked by Oscars. Hood stuck, caught on aircraft bailing out, landed in sea north of Bassein. Handed over to Japs by Burmese. Got medical treatment for severe burns in Bassein. Put into Rangoon City Jail on 12/9/43 then to Rangoon Central Prison on 7/27/44.

1076

Almand, Paul E. 1LT. 0-494774 - Macon, Georgia
99 Squadron, 29 Group, C-46, Pilot.
On 11/7/43 ran supplies India to China, got lost and bailed out south of Myitkyina, walked for 7 days on "D" rations. No water for 3 days. Burmese were tracking me with dogs but managed to evade them. Found some water in bamboo. Shortly was captured in Burmese village and taken to Japs chained in Burmese cart. Taken to city jail 12/1/43. Transferred to Rangoon Central Prison on 7/27/44, in cellblock 5, cell #24. Rest of crew in compound #6.

1077

Maloney, Raymond A. 1LT. 0-726056 - Virgin, Utah.
1 0th Air Force, 9th Bomb Squadron, 7th Bomb Group, B-24, Bombardier.

On 12/1/43 we bombed Ensein. Attacked by I45's, Oscars, Tojos in a 45 minute fight. Bailed out N.W. of Bassein. Burmese gave me to Japs. Ill treated at interrogation. 12/9/43 put in City Jail then to Rangoon Central Prison on 7/27/44, cellblock 5, cell #29.

1078

Baker, Burdett E. 2LT. 0-169884 - Osceola, PA.

491st Squadron, Pilot. Monywa

1079

Walker, Stewart B. 2LT. 0-687461 - Los Angeles, California.

528th Squadron, 3 1 1th Fighter Bomber Group, P-5 1, Pilot

On 2/1 5/44 straffed supply dumps. Hit by Ack-Ack northwest of Meiktila, bailed out. Walked for six days on "D" rations, fish, clams and vegetables. Assistance from Burmese, until they handed me over to Japs. Ill treated at interrogation as I was tied to tree for seven days. Taken by train until Beaufighters shot up the train. They had to continue by truck which overturned while traveling. Got some medical treatment at City Jail 3/12/44. Transferred to Rangoon Central Prison 7/27/44 in cellblock 5, cell #22.

1080

Beardslee, Carl M. F/O T-1643 - Elmira, New York.

459th Fighter Squadron, P-38, Pilot.

On 3/1 1/44 straffed Hemo, attacked by Oscars, on fire. Hit tail as I bailed out. Was unconscious for five days with no memory of opening chute. 3/17/44 I was sent to Rangoon City Jail by air. Then to Rangoon Central Prison 7/27/44, cellblock 5, cell #18.

1084

Wilson, Joe O. let. 0-665257 - Foreman, Arkansas.

529th Bomb Squadron, 311th Bomb Group, P-51, Pilot

On 6/21/44 strafed railway north of Mandalay. Had engine failure, caught fire, had to bail out. Burmese handed me over to Japs. Then taken to Rangoon City Jail on 8/15/44. Severe illness followed by 31 days of loss of memory. Transferred to Rangoon Central Prison on 9/22/44. Cellblock 5, cell #22.

1087

Bray, Clifton L. let. 0-664956 - ElPaso, Texas.

530th Bomb Squadron, 311th Fighter / Bomber Group, P-51, Pilot.

On 5/22/44 we were on a fire sweep in central Burma. Engine caught fire and had to bail out at 300 feet. Chute opened at tree tops. My right arm and leg caught in shroud lines. Walked east for 7 days on 3 rations. Handed over to Japs by Burmese. Severe ill treatment at interrogation at Malar. No medical attention. Was in small cell in Maymyo for 11 weeks with 9 others, all native criminals. Taken to Rangoon City Jail on 8/22/44. Then to Rangoon Central Prison on 9/27/44. Cellblock 5, cell #12.

1091

Bearden, Aaron L. let. 0-748524 - Houston, Texas. 459th Squadron, P-38 Pilot

On 9/3/44 Dropped bombs on Myting Bridge and rammed other P-38. Bailed out and was captured by Burmese and handed over to Japs in Mandalay. Slight ill treatment at interrogation for 4 days, talked bull. Rangoon City Jail 9/14/44. Leg wounded but no medical attention until taken to Rangoon Central Prison 9/22/44 in Cellblock 5, cell #29.

1099

Moore, Richard D. 2Lt. 0-766627 - Des Moines, Iowa.

459th Squadron, P-38 Pilot

On 9/8/44 dropped bombs on Monywa. Flew into ack-ack causing a forced landing. Captured by Burmese and handed over to Japs. Cell was 10' X 12' with B-girl aged 17 years was whimpering for four days. Japs try to crack U.S.A. morals. Burmese spy suspects in other cells also. Rough interrogation at Monywa then on to Shwebo. Better treatment. Japs took precautions against lynching. Transferred to Rangoon Central Prison on 10/14/44.

1100

Engel, Daren C. SGT. 19171011 - Springfield, Oregon

10th Air Force, 83rd Squadron, 12th Bomb Group. B-25 Tail Gunner. On 10/6/44 was bombing bridge at Meiktila when attached by Oscars. On fire, bailed out... two known survivors. Evaded Burmese one day then captured by Burmese then handed over to Japs. Slight burns, little medical treatment after four days. Ill treatment at interrogation at Rangoon prison 10/14/44.

In Cellblock 5, cell #51.

1101

Russel, John L. CPL. 11069380 - Dedham, Massachusetts

10th Air Force, 83rd Squadron, 12th Bomb Group. B-25 Right Gunner. Bullet wound in leg, bailed out, only Daren Engel and I survived. Attacked by Oscar on the way down. Burmese handed me over to Japs. Kicked wounded leg at interrogation, ill medical treatment. Met Engel at Hdqt., then on to Rangoon Central Prison. Cellblock 5, cell #51.

1106

Foley, Michael F. 32382310 - Ithica, New York

490th Bomb Squadron. B-25 Engineer. On 10/16/44 bombed Schwebo Drome, low level inst. bombs. Low cloud cover, hit our own burst. Bailed out, spent one night in jungle. Burmese handed me over to Japs. Malaria, Good treatment at Schwebo. Ill treatment by two drunk officers at Rangoon Central Prison. Cellblock 5. cell #7.

1108

Weesner, Hilton D. 2LT. 0-812179 - South Bend, Indiana

P-47. On 11/12/44 strafing Meiktila, ground fire forced landing. Head injury, regained consciousness in Burmese cart, they handed me over to Japs. Ill treated at interrogation. Taken to Rangoon Central Prison on 11/19/44, got medical treatment. Block 5, cell #53.

1111

Drummey, Robert 1LT. 0-815670 - Boston, Massachusetts.

490th Squadron, B-25 pilot. On 10/16/44 bailed out north of Kalewa. Captured by Japs and taken to Rangoon Central Prison 12/6/44, Cellblock 5, cell #56. Died on 1/12/45 of Malaria and lack of treatment.

1112

Davis, Billy T. 1LT. 0-751226 - Burley, Idaho

58th Squadron. On 11/15/44 strafed North Schwebo, collided with wing man, bailed out. Watched Burmese (priest) one day. Treachery captured by Japs. Very good treatment at Rangoon Central Prison on 12/16/44. Cellblock 5, cell #56.

1114

Paul, Chester E. 1LT. 0-807505 - Laurelton, N.Y.City

45th Bomb Squadron, 40th Bomb Group, B-29 Co-Pilot. Rangoon Central Prison. On 12/16/44, Cellblock 5, cell #61

1115

Parmelee, David B. 2LT. 0-864755 - Guilford, Conn.

45th Bomb Squadron, 45th Bomb Group, B-29 Flight Engineer. Rangoon Central Prison on 12/16/44, cellblock 5, cell #62.

1116

Coffin, Lional F. 1LT. 0-751537 - Duluth, Minnesota

58th Bomb Wing, 40th Bomb Group, 25th Bomb Squadron. Co-Pilot B-29 12/14/44 in Rangoon City Jail then to Rangoon Central Prison on 12/16/44, Cellblock 5, cell #63

1117

Larsen, Norman 2LT. 0-690454 - Brooklyn, New York

20th Bomber Command, 40th Bomb Group, 45th Bomb Squadron. Navigator on B-29.

Dropped bombs over target, hit and on fire, bailed out, shot at from ground, landed in river 300yds from Rangoon City Jail. 12/14/44 in Rangoon City Jail then to Rangoon Central Prison 12/16/44. Cellblock 5, cell #62.

1118

Brooks, Richard M. SGT. 31276801 - Hartford, Connecticut

20th Bomber Command, 40th Bomb Group, 45th Bomb Squadron. Radio Operator on B-29.

Dropped bombs over target, hit and on fire, bailed out, shot at from ground, 400yds from Rangoon City Jail. 12/14/44 in Rangoon City Jail, then to Rangoon Central Prison on 12/16/44. Cellblock 5, cell #62.

1119

Thomasian, Karnig A. SGT.12183215 Manhattan, N.Y.C.

20th Air Force, 20th Bomber Command, 40th Bomb Group, 45th Bomb Squadron.

Left Gunner, Electrical Specialist. On 12/14/44 Rangoon was our secondary target. We had just dropped bombs when there was a tremendous explosion that blew our formation apart. Plane went down in a flat spin with three engines blazing and no controls working. Bailed out and was immediately captured by Burmese and Japs. Taken to City Jail, interrogated, beaten. Two days later we were all transferred to the Rangoon Central Prison 12/16/44 to cellblock 5, cell #62.

1120

Edwards, Francis R. SGT. 32381707 - Cuba, New York.

20th Bomber Command, 40th Bomb Group, 25th Bomb Squadron. CFC Gunner on B-29.

Dropped bombs over target, hit and on fire, bailed out, 12/14/44 in Rangoon City Jail then to Rangoon Central Prison on 12/16/44. Cellblock 5, cell #61.

1121

Dow, Stanton L. S/SGT. 11122246 - Gardiner, Maine.

20th Bomber Command, 40th Bomb Group, 45th Bomb Squadron. Gunner on B-29.

Dropped bombs over target, hit and on fire, bailed out, landed on small island southeast of Rangoon. Picked up by Burmese and handed over to Japs. 12/14/44 in Rangoon City Jail then to Rangoon Central Prison on

12/16/44. Cellblock 5, cell #61.

1122

Trinkner, Edward F. T/SGT. 1205851 - Bronx, New York
20th Bomber Command, 40th Bomb Group, 45th Bomb Squadron. On B-29.
Dropped bombs over target, hit and on fire, bailed out, 12/14/44 in Rangoon City Jail then to Rangoon Central Prison on 12/16/44. Cellblock 5, cell #61.

1123

Meyer, Cornelius C. Captain 0-383620 -
58th Bomb Wing, 40th Bomb Gp., 25th Bomb Sq. Pilot B-29.
Moments after dropping bombs a tremendous explosion under the formation caused a major disaster. Our plane out of control, bailed out and quickly captured by Japs. 12/14/44 taken to a Jap Army Post then to Rangoon Central Prison on 12/16/44. Cellblock 5, cell #63.

1124

McGivern, James B. 2LT. 0-690465 - Staples, Minnesota
20th Bomber Command, 40th Bomb Group, 45th Bomb Squadron. Bombardier on B-29.
Dropped bombs on target, hit and on fire, bailed out, caught by Japs 12/14/44 in Rangoon City Jail then to Rangoon Central Prison on 12/16/44. Cellblock 5, cell #63.

1125

Whitley, Charles W. M/SGT. 14049026 - Charlotte, North Carolina
Arrived Rangoon Central Prison 12/15/44
Cellblock 5, cell #63.

1126

Walsh, William J. 1LT. 0-863805 - Boston, Mass.

Arrived Rangoon Central Prison 12/19/44, Cellblock 5, cell #64.

1127

Burke, Marion B. 1LT. 0-731436 - Tampa, Florida

58th Bomb Wing, 40th Bomb Group,25th Bomb Squadron Navigator B-29. Moments after dropping bombs a tremendous explosion under the formation caused a major disaster. Our plane out of control, bailed out and quickly captured by Japs. 12/14/44 taken to a Japanese Army Post then to Rangoon Central Prison on 12/16/44. Cellblock 5, cell 64.

1128

Derrington, Robert CAPT. 0-737550 - Detroit, Michigan

58th Bomb Wing, 40th Bomb Group, 25th Bomb Squadron. (Observer) Pilot B-29.

(Same as #1127) Cellblock 5, cell #64.

1129

Levine, Joseph 1LT. 0-811683 - Brooklyn, New York

58th Bomb Wing, 40th Bomb Group, 25th Bomb Squadron. Navigator B-29. (Same as # 1127) Cellblock 5, cell #64.

1130

Montgomery, Richard A. M/SGT. 7022868 - Pittsburgh, Pennsylvania

58th Bomb Wing, 40th Bomb Group, 25th Bomb Squadron. Radio Operator B-29. (Same #1127) Left hand severed at wrist in aircraft. Bailed out and landed in a rice paddy and quickly captured by Burmese and given to Japs. Gave himself shot of morphine from his kit. Others from his crew were captured and they helped to give him one more shot of morphine. Due to insufficient medical treatment, amputation was necessary, Japs botched the job and a second amputation was done by a British doctor on 12/30/44 successfully. Followed by the barest medical treatment. Cellblock 5, cell #64

1134
Greene, Harlan B. S/SGT. 32475333 - Belmont, N.Y.
20th Bomber Command, 40th Bomb Group, 45th Bomb Squadron. Gunner on B-29.
Dropped bombs on target, we were hit, headed west for 30 min., started losing altitude, bailed out. Burmese gave us some food then gave us to Japs. Entered Rangoon Central Prison on 12/23/44, Cellblock 5, cell #66.

1136
Shanks, Robert C. CAPT. 0-1699413 - Grand Prarie, Texas
20th Bomber Command, 40th Bomb Group, 45th Bomb Squadron. Pilot on B-29.
Dropped bombs on target, we were hit, headed west for 30 min., started losing altitude, bailed out. Burmese gave us some food then gave us to Japs. Entered Rangoon Central Prison on 12123/44, Cellblock 5, cell #66.

1137
Fletcher, Harold E. 1LT. 0-806317 - Beardstown, Illinois
20th Bomber Command, 40th Bomb Group, 45th Bomb Squadron. Co-Pilot on B-29.
Sprained ankle, medical treatment, beaten by Burmese (Same account as #1136)

1138

Cochran, Julian C. 2LT. 0-683118 - Fort Scott, Kansas
20th Bomber Command, 40th Bomb Group, 45th Bomb Squadron.
Navigator on B-29. (Same account as # 1136)

1139

Benedict, Cameron R. 2LT. 0-684602 - Elmira, New York
20th Bomber Command, 40th Bomb Group, 45th Bomb Squadron.
Bombardier on B-29. (Same account as #1136) Very good treatment by
Karens.

1140

Etherington, Galpin M. 2LT. 0-863760 - Los Angelis, California
20th Bomber Command, 40th Bomb Group, 45th Bomb Squadron.
Engineer on B-29.
On 12/14/44, immediately after the release of bombs, there was a
tremendous explosion in the air below us and whole formation dispersed
in all directions. Flew for about 20 minutes then had to bail out. Landed
near a small village and soon given over to the Japs. Eleven days later, on
Christmas day we arrived at the Rangoon Central Prison and placed in
Cellblock 5, cell #67.

1141

Pisterzi, Henry T/SGT. 18069493 - Denver, Colorado
20th Bomber Command, 40th Bomb Group, 45th Bomb Squadron. Tail
Gunner on B-29. (Same account as #1140)

1142

Lentz. Walter R. S/SGT. 34433023 - Stony Point, North Carolina
20th Bomber Command, 40th Bomb Group, 45th Bomb Squadron.

R.Gunner on B-29.

(Same account as # 1136) Cellblock 5, cell #67.

1143

Sommers, Lewis W. S/SGT. 35589579 - Martins Ferry, Ohio

20th Bomber Command, 40th Bomb Group, 45th Bomb Squadron. Radar Operator on B-29.

(Same account as #1136) Cellblock 5, cell #67.

1144

Basche, Arnold S/SGT. 37263497 Sioux Falls, S. Dakota

20th Bomber Command, 40th Bomb Group, 45th Bomb Squadron. L. Gunner on B-29.

(Same account as # 1136) Cellblock 5, cell #68.

1145

Majors, Ferrell T. S/SGT. 39273801 - Los Angeles, California

20th Bomber Command, 40th Bomb Group, 45th Bomb Squadron. Radio Operator on B-29.

(Same account as # 1136) Cellblock 5, cell #68.

1146

Oglesby, Nicholas P. S/SGT. 13118908 - Charlottesville, Virginia

20th Bomber Command, 40th Bomb Group, 45th Bomb Squadron. CFC Gunner B-29.

(Same account as # 1136) Cellblock 5, cell #68.

USAAF DIED IN CAPTIVITY OR MISSING IN ACTION

LT. Lockett, Robert L. Wichita Falls, Texas. 311 F.B. Squadron
On 11/25/43 (told by Japs) He was found dead in aircraft. AGO picture
verification.

COL. Melton, H.R. Kentucky - C.O. 311 Fighter Bomber Group. On
11/25/43 bailed out north of Bassein area on way back from Rangoon.
To Rangoon City Jail then to Rangoon Central Prison
for one month. Removed fairly fit sing ? 1/9/44

CAPT. Billwright Commerce, Texas. 7th Bomb Group, Pilot of B-24
On 12/1/43 bombing Rangoon was hit by Oscars - bailed out near
Bassein, walked one week - Burmese took him to Japs. Entered Rangoon
City Jail 12/13/43. Died 3/31/44 as a result of beating with club for
picking up cigar butt. Hit on top of backbone. Two days later died reading
bible. Otherwise fit, no complaints, big bruise.
Nine of B-24 crew shot down by Oscars near Bassein after bombing
Insein on 12/1/43. LT. Erwin, E.W. survived. 7th Bomb Group. New
crew in India five days.

2LT. Carpenter-Pilot, B-24, 2LT. Clybourn, C.A. - Bombardier who
bailed out and was strafed on the way down. Compound fracture of leg.
Believed died Bassein Hospital.
Nine of crew of B-24. Rammed by Oscar when crippled near Bodie after
bombing Rangoon ships on 10/26/43. LT. Vaughan - Pilot, 2LT. Waller
who also bailed out. Fate unknown.

LT.Zizlowski, Joseph F.- Bombardier, B-25 - New Buffalo, Michigan. AA fire over Monywa. M.B.GP. bailed out 75 miles Northwest of Monywa, uninjured. 12/19/43. With Redd, Rangoon City Jail, 1/17/44. Died dysentery, malnutrition 7/20/44. No medical treatment, Rats...toes.

2LT. Baker, Burdett - Pilot. New York. Oscars...Bailed out 12/14/43, injured ribs, foot. No medical treatment in Rangoon City Jail 1/14/44. Amebic dysentery in Rangoon Central Prison 7/27/44. Died 11/23/44 from dysentery and malnutrition. Four others went in with aircraft:

2LT. Simonic, Co-Pilot, his chute got caught on the vertical stabilizer. S/SGT. Buckfield, M., Radio/Gunner, S/SGT. Murphy, Top Gunner .

S/Sgt. Quick, Ernest S. - Miami, Florida - 7th Bomb Group, Radio Operator on B-24.
Shot down on 11/14143. Grady Farley and I were the only ones to get out of the plane. The eight that died are: Pilot, LT. Kimball, George / Co-Pilot, Johnson / Flt/Officer George / Bombardier, 2LT. Walker, Albert, Mississippi. / 2LT. Liebonitz, Hyman -New York. / Engineer S/SGT. Becker, William C. - Ohio. / Gunner S/SGT. Callahan, Paul B.- North Carolina / Gunner S/SGT. Speck Karl S. -Kansas / Gunner S/SGT. Cory - Washington State.

10 of crew of B-24 shot down 11/17/43. 3 died with aircraft, 8 bailed out, 5 straffed in air from 14,000 / 6,000 feet. 3 survived jump. Bombardier LT. Butterfield, Royal W. -Daney, Nebraska. Wounded two places, no medical treatment. Stick recovered but died of beri-beri at Rangoon City Jail, 4/24/44, no medical treatment / Navigator 2LT. Rich, J.C. - Portland, Maine. Burns, no medical treatment. Recovered but died of amebic dysentery, scabies and beri-beri (80 lbs) 9/13/44 Rangoon Central

Prison. Others are:lLT. Meredith - Pilot / Co-Pilot - 2LT. Ryan, E.F. - New York / Gunner / Pilot 2LT. Stephens, T.M. - Indianapolis, Indiana / Radar S/SGT. Temples, E.W. -Georgia. / Engineer- S/SGT. Smeal,T.H. -Pennsylvania. / RadioOperatorS/SGT. Hart, F.W. - New York. / Gunner -SGT. Cook, J.H. - Montana / GunnerSGT. Pers C.E. - New York. / S/SGT. Rodriquez, Oakland, California. (See 1045

S/SGT. Sheets - Harrisburg, Pennsylvania - Pilot L5, lost, landed in Chindwin River and sank. Died Rangoon Central Prison on 11/11/44, delayed concussion or heartbreak.

CAPT. Gillhouse, Wm. - Des Moine, Iowa. 1 st A/coms, P-5 1. 5/18/44 Karin ground fire, on fire had to bail out. 6/6/44 Burns, no medical treatment at Rangoon City Jail. Died 7/26/44 wouldn't eat....off head.

1LT. Stom, Franklyn J. - Evanston, Illinois - Navigator. Died Schwebu Jail, 12/2/44 of malaria and no medical treatment. Radio Operator afraid to Bail out, crashed with aircraft, name not known. Gunner bailed out not heard from since, name not known.

S/SGT. Winderl, Francis C. - Montana. - 9th Bomb Squadron, Radio Operator. 12/1/43 while bombing Bassein was hit by Oscars. Seen to bail out, nothing heard from since.

S/SGT. Girman, E.T. - Indiana. - Waist Gunner.
Bailed out, nothing heard from since.

1LT. Parker, Merryl -Harrisburgh, Pennsylvania - Co-Pilot, bailed out. Signal shots...heard nothing since.

LT. Couch - 83rd Squadron, Pilot B-25. On 10/6/44, died or missing, also Co-Pilot, name not known. LT. Mauldin, George - Bombardier/Navigator - Texas. SGT. Wilson, engineer, burned in turret, hit by bullets. One of above seen to bail out with no trace.

1LT. Kaufman, Richard - Wyoming - 9th Bomb Squadron, Pilot B-24. On 4/5/44 shot in stomach in aircraft and died immediately. 1LT. Pittman - Saved lives of crew who bailed out by pulling aircraft up so they could jump. He and LT. James, Alex - Navigator, crashed with aircraft along with T/SGT. Faulkner - Georgia - Engineer., T/SGT. Ball - Radio Operator, SGT. Harris E.J. - Tail Gunner, S/SGT. Shultz, Melvin Nose Gunner, CAPT. Dorst, Observer - Bailed out, seen alive on ground, empty chute found but not heard of since.

LT. Boldman, Amil - Costa Mesa, California - 459th Squadron, Pilot P-38. On 4/6/44 strafed Heno. Two Oscars attached, hit, bailed out. Strafed on way down. Hurt stomach, Burmese took me to Japs in Meiktila City Jail 4/15/44 by air. Died 7/16/44 of malnutrition and ill treatment.

1sLT. Treimer, Wayne "Doc"
Pilot B-29. On 12/14/44 after dropping bombs on Rangoon Rail Station, there was a terrific explosion under the formation and his plane flipped over and the righted itself from the impact and went directly into a flat spin within a spin with 3 engines in flames and no controls. Finally it hit the ground in a burst of fire and explosion. He stayed with the plane to try to give the crew time to bail out.

CPL. Henning, Vernon. Central Fire Control Gunner on B-29. On 12/14/44 after dropping bombs on Rangoon Rail Station, there was a terrific explosion under the formation and his plane flipped over and the righted itself from the impact and went directly into a flat spin within a spin with three engines in flames and no controls. Finally it hit the ground in a burst of fire and explosion. Vernon was unable to get out in time.

CPL. McCutcheon, Leon. Right Gunner/Engine Mechanic on B-29.
On 12/14/44 after dropping bombs on Rangoon Rail Station, there was a terrific explosion under the formation and his plane flipped over and the righted itself from the impact and went directly into a flat spin within a spin with three engines in flames and no controls. Finally it hit the ground in a burst of fire and explosion. Leon was unable to get out in time.

CPL. Harmison, August "Augie". Tail Gunner on B-29
On 12/14/44 after dropping bombs on Rangoon Rail Station, there was a terrific explosion under the formation and his plane flipped over and the righted itself from the impact and went directly into a flat spin within a spin with three engines in flames and no controls. Finally it hit the ground in a burst of fire and explosion. Augie was unable to get out in time.

CPL. Dalton, Robert. Radar Operator on B-29
On 12/14/44 after dropping bombs on Rangoon Rail Station, there was a terrific explosion under the formation and his plane flipped over and the righted itself from the impact and went directly into a flat spin within a spin with three engines in flames and no controls. Finally hit the ground in a burst of fire and explosion. Bob was unable to get out in time.

FINIS

ABOUT THE AUTHOR

A New Yorker, Karnig Thomasian volunteered for the Army Air Corp in 1942 at the age of 18. As a left gunner on a B-29 Superfortress during WWII he fought against the Japanese.

After his liberation as a prisoner of war, and an honorable discharge from the service, Thomasian used the GI Bill to attend the Art Students League in New York. He worked in top advertising agencies and a graphic design firm for the next 44 years.

Retirement in 1996 enabled him to pursue his artistic capabilities, however his deepest desire was to help ex-pows / veterans in getting their disability compensations. He became an accredited National Service Officer in 1999 and to this day, has helped over 236 combat veterans.

Cover Design by Karnig Thomasian

Computer Graphics by Janet Kroenke

CPSIA information can be obtained at www.ICGtesting.com
Printed in the USA
BVOW04s0313071016

464269BV00008B/8/P